19

Typography 19

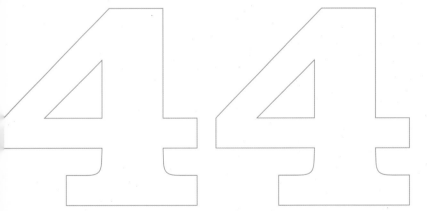

Watson-Guptill Publications, New York

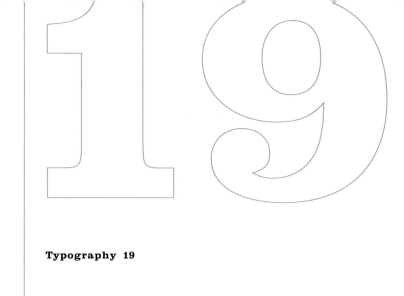

Typography 19

The Annual of the Type Directors Club 44th Exhibition

First published in 1998
in the United States by
Watson-Guptill Publications,
a division of
BPI Communications, Inc.,
1515 Broadway,
New York, N.Y. 10036

The Library of Congress has
cataloged this serial title as follows:
Typography (Type Directors Club [U.S.])
Typography: the annual of the
Type Directors Club.—/—
New York: Watson-Guptill Publications,
1980–
v.ill; 29 cm

Annual.
ISSN 0275-6870 = Typography
(New York, N.Y.)
1. Printing, Practical—Periodicals.
2. Graphic arts—periodicals.
1. Type Directors Club (U.S.)
z243.A2T9a 686.2'24 81-640363
AACR 2 MARC-S
Library of Congress [8605]

Manufactured in Hong Kong

ISBN 0-8230-5554-X

1 2 3 4 5 / 02 01 00 99 98

Acknowledgments

The Type Directors Club gratefully
acknowledges the following for their
support and contributions to the
success of TDC44 and TDC[2]:

Design: L. Richard Poulin, Amy Kwon,
     Poulin + Morris
Exhibition facilities:
     The Arthur A. Houghton, Jr. Gallery,
     The Cooper Union
Judging facilities: School of Visual Arts
Chairmen's and judges' photos:
     Keith Trumbo
Photography of selected entries:
     Jelly Bean Photographic
     Jan Pivoda/Show & Tell

TDC44 competition (call for entries):
Design: Poulin + Morris
Printer: The Perlmuter Printing Company
Paper: sappi/S. D. Warren Company
Separations: Tana Color Graphics, Inc.
Photography: Lisa Spindler, Graphistock

TDC[2] competition (call for entries):
Design and typography: James Montalbano
     and Paul Shaw
Printer: Phototype Color Graphics
Film: A to A Graphic Services, Inc.
Paper: sappi/S. D. Warren Company

For Watson-Guptill Publications:
Senior Editor: Marian Appellof
Associate Editor: Alison Hagge
Design Coordinator: Jay Anning
Production Manager: Ellen Greene

The principal typefaces used
in the composition of *Typography 19*
are Berthold Clarendon, Monotype
Grotesque, and Sabon.

Contents

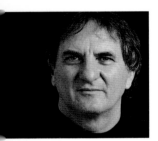

Richard Wilde is the chairman of both
the Graphic Design and the Advertising
Departments at the School of Visual Arts.
Wilde is an art director and graphic
designer; a senior vice president of graphic
design at Ryan Drossman & Partners, Inc.
where his clients include J. P. Morgan,
TDK, MovieFone, Bear Stearns, Wildman
& Sons, Fuji Water, and Arm & Hammer;
and a principal of Wilde Design. He has
written and designed *Problems/Solutions:
Visual Thinking for Graphic
Communications* and co-authored with
Judith Wilde both *Visual Literacy* and
101 Ways to Stay Young. Wilde's work has
been published in *Graphis* and *Creativity*
as well as in the annuals of the New York
Art Directors Club, Graphis, American
Institute of Graphic Arts, Print, One Show,
Andy Awards, Society of Illustrators,
Society of Publication Designers, and the
Type Directors Club. His work also
appeared in *Print* magazine, *Print
Casebooks*, *Critique*, *Idea* magazine, *Art
Direction*, *U&lc*, *Vision*, and *HOW*. Wilde
has received more than 100 awards includ-
ing the Art Directors Club of New York,
Andys, Type Directors Club, The American
Institute of Graphic Arts, Society of
Illustrators, The One Club, *Critique*,
Communication Arts, *Print Casebooks*,
Creativity, and the Society of Publication
Designers. Wilde is an international
lecturer and creator of experimental
design workshops throughout the U.S.,
Canada, Asia, Europe, and South America.
Wilde has been chairman of the TDC
Program Committee for the past two years
and TDC44 chairman for the past year.
He is currently on the board of the
New York Art Directors Club and is the
New York editor of *HOW*.

Richard Wilde, Chairman

The definition of typographic excellence is constantly expanding. It has
gotten to the point that even illegibility, once considered the kiss of death,
is commonplace. In counterculture expression, this form serves as content
that defines Generation X. This sensibility—as well as other Generation X
expressions such as rap music, which caused much debate concerning its
volatility—has now become an art form. With this in mind, the difficulty for
me as the judging chair of TDC44 was to find judges who were sympathetic
to this aesthetic, as well as to the old, the classical, the avant-garde, the
traditional, the retro, the conceptual, and the formalistic, while at the same
time were open, civil, constructively confrontational, and accepting of one
another's conceits and opinions so as to embrace the diversity of typographic
excellence. In short, the result was a team of diverse professionals:
Henrietta Condak, Stacy Drummond, Michael Ian Kaye, Jeffrey Metzner,
Hideki Nakajima, L. Richard Poulin, and Neil Powell. Each with a distinct
point of view, the judges' combined standards were so demanding that the
number of selected winning entries totaled but 168, the lowest number in
recent TDC history. The standards of these 168 works will set the typographic
criteria by which to measure excellence.

Henrietta Condak

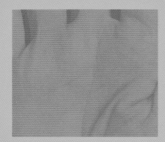

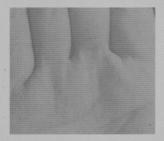

Hideki Nakajima

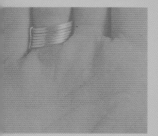

Michael Ian Kaye

L. Richard Poulin

Neil Powell

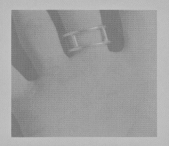

TDC44 Judges

Jeffrey Metzner

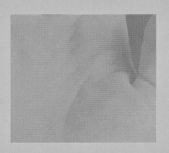

Stacy Drummond

Judges

Henrietta Condak

Henrietta Condak is an art director, graphic designer, and a graduate of The Cooper Union. Her work has received numerous awards as well as recognition from the Art Directors Club in New York, the Society of Illustrators, and the American Institute of Graphic Arts. Her work has been published in all the leading design publications and journals in the United States and abroad. She was the senior art director of the Masterworks label at Columbia Records. After leaving CBS she opened her own design studio, and continues to produce work for a wide variety of publishing, entertainment, and corporate clients. Condak teaches design and typography at the School of Visual Arts in New York.

CHOPIN

RICHARD GOODE

POLONAISE - FANTAISIE

SCHERZO NO. 4

NOCTURNE OP. 55 NO. 2

5 MAZURKAS

BARCAROLLE

Turn the phone off, lock the door, put the cat out, turn off any bright lights, recline in a comfortable position, and allow yourself to relax. As you begin to listen, you may wish to set the intention for healing by visualizing and "sensualizing," experiencing with as many senses as possible, that which you want healed. ☮ Allow the sound to carry you very deep inside yourself where you can float in a state of regeneration, rest and peace. If you start to emerge from your state of deep relaxation before the end of this section, simply focus on the music once again and allow yourself to be carried back down. Notice how you feel inside yourself when you are gt your most relaxed and begin to recreate those feelings inside. If you "disappear" or lose conscious awareness during "the deep," don't worry. The healing state can continue inside until you are reawakened at the end. ☮ As the music arouses you toward the end of the piece, allow yourself once again to "sensualize" the healing, this time seeing it as if it had already taken place. Visualize yourself as already healed. Look into the future and imagine a situation where you would normally have been affected or limited by the illness, and experience yourself as being completely well and fully functioning. Allow yourself to reawaken, feeling alert, refreshed and present. Take several deep breaths and stretch fully before sitting or standing and continuing your day.

Stacy Drummond

Stacy Drummond is currently responsible for the creative direction of packaging and advertising at Tommy Boy Music. She joined Tommy Boy in 1996. Before joining Tommy Boy, she was with Sony Music for 13 years. She was the design director for Columbia Records and Legacy for six years and art director for the prior seven years. Drummond has worked with a variety of artists including Coolio, Cyndi Lauper, Cypress Hill, Kris Kross, Indigo Girls, Nneena Freelon, Arthur Blythe, and Russell Malone, to name a few. She has won numerous awards, including a gold medal from the Art Directors Club and a gold medal from The One Club. Other awards include the AIGA, STA100, Print, BDA, and Communication Arts. Drummond is also an instructor at the School of Visual Arts.

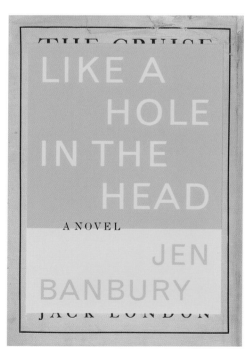

Michael Ian Kaye

Michael Ian Kaye is a creative director at Little, Brown and Company. Formerly the art director of Farrar, Straus and Giroux and an associate art director at Penguin USA, Kaye has designed many books and book jackets. Kaye has also designed issues of *U&lc* for the International Typeface Corporation, *Faces on the Edge: Type in the Digital Age*, and is currently art directing the *AIGA Journal of Graphic Design*. His work has received awards from The American Institute of Graphic Arts, *Print*, *Graphis*, the Art Directors Club, and the Type Directors Club, and has been published in the following annuals: *Covers and Jackets*, *Mixing Messages*, *Print Magazine*, *Type Play*, and *U&lc*. Kaye's work was included in the Cooper-Hewitt National Design Museum's exhibition "Mixing Messages: Graphic Design in Contemporary Culture" and the Art Directors Club's "Young Guns NYC," an exhibit of work by young New York-based designers, illustrators, and photographers. He graduated from the University of Louisville Allen R. Hite Institute in 1987 and teaches at the School of Visual Arts. Mr. Kaye lives in Brooklyn with his dog.

Jeffrey Metzner

Hired by Bates & Co. in 1958 while still in high school, Metzner stayed there to learn the craft of commercial art instead of attending art school. He worked at Y&R, Hobson's Ltd. (London), and McCann Marschalk (now Lowe & Partners), until finding a home at the innovative Doyle Dane Bernbach, where he achieved recognition as their renegade art director. He left DDB to work for his mentor, George Lois, at PKL and later was hired at Daniel & Charles (now Gotham) as creative director. Once at D&C he began directing his own commercials and then left at the age of 29 to start Jeffrey Metzner Productions, an award-winning TV commercial production company that he maintained until 1989. He is now a senior creative director at Avrett Free & Ginsberg and completely diversified as a (completely computer literate) art director, designer, and director. He also teaches an internationally-acclaimed alternative portfolio class at the School of Visual Arts. Over the years Metzner has won numerous awards, including the Art Directors Club Gold Medal in 1978 for a commercial he wrote, art directed, and directed. Metzner is married, with eight children and two grandchildren. He has a small farm in Chatham, New York, a hideaway in Moab, Utah, and lives and works in New York City.

A STARVING ARTIST WILL ALWAYS BE COOLER THAN A WELL-FED ACCOUNTANT

rett, Free & Ginsberg Advertising supports the High School of Art & Design

Hideki Nakajima

Hideki Nakajima is a native of Japan. In 1992 he became an art director for several magazines at Rockin'on Inc. and in 1995 he established Nakajima Design Co. Ltd. Hideki has won seven medals from the Art Directors Club in New York and was a judge in their competition in 1997. His recent works include editorial assignments for *CUT* for Rockin'on, *DUNE*, Mark Borthwick Synthetic Voices, and Elizabeth Payton's book *Live Forever*. Hideki has also done fashion campaigns for PARCO department as well as a CD jacket design for Ryuichi Sakamoto.

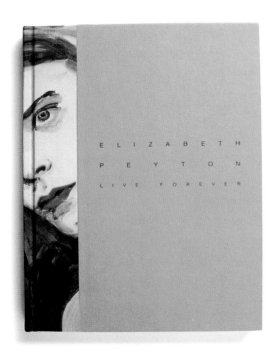

L. Richard Poulin

L. Richard Poulin is a principal of Poulin + Morris, a New York City-based multidisciplinary design consultant firm involved in all facets of visual communications, including graphic design, environmental graphics and architectural sign programs, graphic identity, publication design, interactive electronic media, promotional print, and exhibition design. His clients include Alcoa, Hines, Columbia University, Gwathmey Siegel & Associates, the Indianapolis Museum of Art, Johnson & Johnson, Morgan Stanley, NBC, New York University Medical Center, Polshek and Partners Architects, Sony Music Entertainment, and W. W. Norton & Co. He is presently a faculty member of the School of Visual Arts in New York City and was an adjunct professor at The Cooper Union. Poulin's work has been published in numerous periodicals and books, is in the permanent collection of the Library of Congress, has been exhibited at the Brno International Biennale and the Royal College of Art, and has received awards from *Communication Arts*, *Print Casebooks*, the American Institute of Architects, The American Institute of Graphic Arts, the Art Directors Clubs in New York, Los Angeles, and San Francisco, *Graphis*, *ID*, the Society for Environmental Graphic Design, the Society of Publication Designers, and the Type Directors Club. He has served as President of the New York Chapter of The American Institute of Graphic Arts and is a recipient of a research grant in design history from the Graham Foundation for Advanced Studies in the Fine Arts.

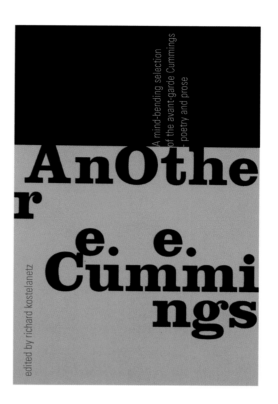

A mind-bending selection of the avant-garde Cummings poetry and prose

AnOther e. e. Cummings

edited by richard kostelanetz

Neil Powell

Neil Powell joined Joe Duffy and his
group as an intern in March 1991,
shortly after graduating with a BFA
from the University of Kentucky. Now,
seven years later, Powell is the design
director of Duffy NYC. Powell's work
includes national and international
branding, corporate identity, and web
site development for clients such as
BMW, Giorgio Armani, Tidy Cat,
The Lee Apparel Company, Jim Beam
Brands, The Stroh Brewery Company,
The Coca-Cola Company, Hart Skis,
Time magazine, and Faith Popcorn's
BrainReserve. Powell's work has been
recognized nationally and internation-
ally in design award shows such as
The American Institute of Graphic
Arts, the Type Directors Club, the
New York Art Directors Club, D&AD,
Communication Arts, *Graphis*, and *I.D.*
magazines. His work is also part of
the permanent collection in the
Cooper-Hewitt National Design
Museum of the Smithsonian
Institution. He has lectured on design
throughout the U.S. Powell is also on
the faculty of the School of Visual
Arts, where he is actively involved in
teaching a senior portfolio class.

TDC44 Judges' Choices and Designers' Statements

Henrietta Condak

The use of type and letterforms as both graphic and textural elements is central to the success of the collages in this stunningly reproduced calendar. The collagist's grasp of the letterform's artistic power and the designer's perception of the collage as calendar art expand the symbiosis of artist/ printer to artist/printer/designer. The designer's challenge was to create a calendar design that would work with these strong typographic collages. She accomplishes this by placing the calendar information on an overlay. In this way, the art retains its integrity while allowing the designer to make a strong typographic statement of her own. Each type design, when viewed through the semi-transparent overlay, merges with the collage to become a useful calendar as well as a dynamic poster. The designer's interesting use of the bar code and the choice of an electronic style typeface are neatly married with the shopping bag themed prints. The message therefore is clear: though we can now shop electronically, we still need to carry our goods in a sturdy bag. Thanks to the designer's regard for the art and bold use of typography, this timeless calendar makes its presence felt.

Kurt Weidemann said of this calendar: "Here Peter Steiner found Franz Wagner: an ideal team of artist and printer. Two compatible talents of whom one sees and creates and the other produces what the first has seen—precisely, almost cloned. The printer did not change one iota, did not reinvent the art. With subtle means and without loss the artistic act was recreated. The term 'art of printing' is truly descriptive of this work. Whoever searches for the pinnacle of graphic arts reproduction can stop right here." Peter Steiner, like Kurt Weidemann, taught at the Academy of Fine Arts in Stuttgart. When Steiner teamed up with serigrapher Franz Wagner, two artistic minds found each other, a symbiosis leading to an extraordinary result. With this calendar, designed by Regina Steiner, freely conceived collages—in their subtle dimensionality on diverse substrates from glossy to tracing paper and imbued with shades normally not attainable in color reproduction—presented extreme challenges to the screen printing process. The concept of omitting the calendariums on the art sheets but printing the type—ITC Weidemann and OCR-A—on preceding, semi-transparent interleafs preserves the artistic value and longevity of the reproductions.
Klaus Schmidt, Type Directors Club

CALENDAR

DESIGN
**Peter and Regina
Steiner**
Stuttgart, Germany

PHOTOGRAPHY
Franz Wagner

TEXT
Kurt Weidemann

CLIENT
Wagner Siebdruck

PRINCIPAL TYPE
**ITC Weidemann
and OCR-A**

DIMENSIONS
**$18^{7}/_{8}$ x $27^{1}/_{8}$ in.
(48 x 69 cm)**

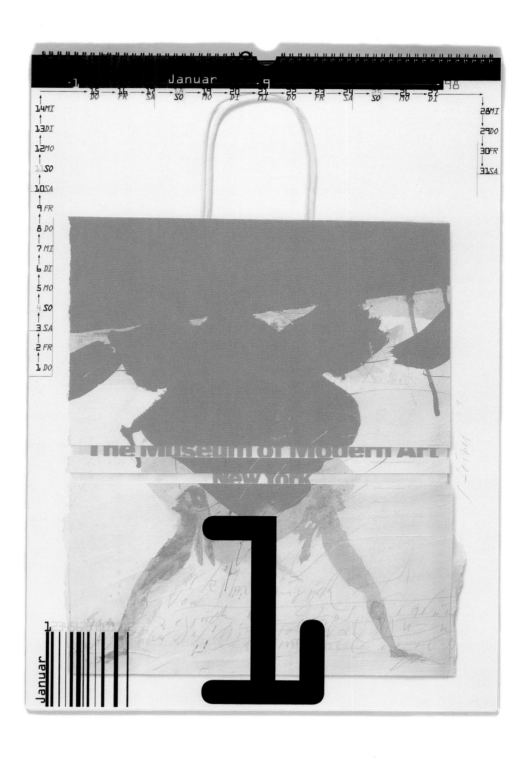

Stacy Drummond

In tribute to the minimalism of this poster, I am going to make this statement brief. Neither the typography nor the graphic design is competing for individual attention. Quite the contrary. They are working in complete harmony. The message the poster is communicating is not clouded with arbitrary, trendy typography. The typography actually returns to a time when clarity and respect for the image were paramount. I would like to thank the designer for having had the courage to execute such a clear vision.

This is an appeal poster for the United Nations Framework Convention on Climate Change. The broken space in the center represents the earth, and it expresses my mind, which is weak for the destruction of the environment.

"Let's talk before it's too late."

"Let's act before it's too late."

I will continue to appeal to the above messages.

Akio Okumura

POSTER

DESIGN
Aki Inoue
Osaka, Japan

ART DIRECTION
Akio Okumura

CREATIVE DIRECTION
Akio Okumura

DESIGN OFFICE
Packaging Create, Inc.

CLIENT
**Kyoto Committee
for the Environmental
Poster Design
Exhibition '97**

PRINCIPAL TYPE
**Univers Light and
Helvetica Narrow Bold**

DIMENSIONS
**$28^{5}/_{8}$ x $40^{9}/_{16}$ in.
(72.8 x 103 cm)**

Michael Ian Kaye

My Judge's Choice selection was much easier to make than I had anticipated it would be. I selected a piece that I had sought out independent of my Type Directors Club affiliation, and so had already devoted several hours to the Hirst/Barnbrook experience. I was excited that this book had been submitted because I had already deemed it to be one of the most exciting design projects of 1997. Art and design unite on the page with a sense of humor and intelligence that is unprecedented in the artist monograph genre. Barnbrook's attention to detail, his superb craftsmanship, and his typographic savvy keep this project in the realm of serious design and protect it from being written off as gratuitous or of the moment. The layering of words, images, and ideas are done in a way that makes every spread tell a story, answer a question or ask several—making the viewer a participant. It is truly rare when a piece of design works on so many levels, yet remains pure and accessible.

It's amazing that the art world, which is supposed to be the lifeblood of culture, is generally so conservative when it comes to the design of books. The Damien Hirst book was an attempt to address a few of these problems. Above all I tried to make it fun, to say art does deal with big things but it can also be irreverent and fun (the book features interactive pop-ups and pullouts). I also tried to make it readable with small chunks of text rather than a huge slab of "academic gray," which most people do not read. A strong graphic treatment, which was a direct response to the concepts of the artist, was used throughout, as putting large images on a white page does not make them easier to see or understand.
Jonathan Barnbrook

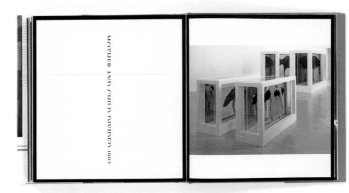

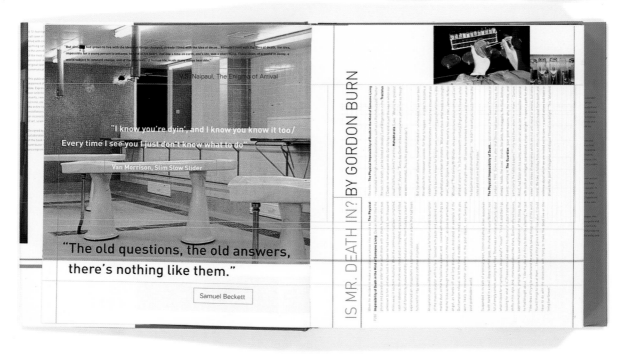

Hideki Nakajima

The Damien Hirst book, "I want to spend The Rest of My Life Everywhere, with Everyone, One to One, Always, Forever, Now," showed new horizons—not only of typography but of art direction and book design. Generally, when we design an "art book," we try not to have strong graphics on the art works. We try to show the art works as they are. Not to destroy the works, we do not crop them, we keep the credit as small as possible, and we put the works in order. That is a very traditional and fair way of designing an art book. However, this book is totally going the other way. We see graphic design *on* the works, and works are shown in different sizes and in different orders. The colors of the backgrounds and typography destroy the works. The letters are in different fonts and page numbers are put in different ways. We see very old-fashioned and no cool typography. In addition, there are pop-ups, pullouts, etc. These devices usually destroy the works, but in this book amazingly everything is in splendid harmony. This marvelous book design shows the first and absolutely the most sophisticated way to design an art book, releasing us from old, conservative boundaries and restrictions. We used to attempt to make a book to show the works as simply as possible. However, this book proves that the art works themselves and the art book can be totally different things. Finally, without a close and respectful relationship between Damien Hirst and Jonathan Barnbrook, this would not have happened. It says "One Plus One Equals Three."

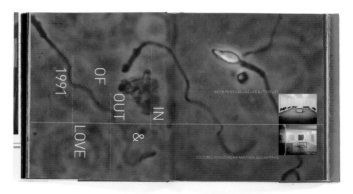

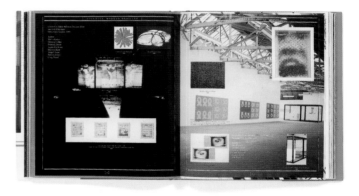

BOOK

DESIGN
Jonathan Barnbrook
London, England

ART DIRECTION
Jonathan Barnbrook

DESIGN ASSISTANCE
Jason Beard

CLIENT
Booth-Clibborn Editions

PRINCIPAL TYPE
DIN

DIMENSIONS
13 x 11⁷/₁₆ in. (33 x 29 cm)

Founded by forward-thinking graduates of the MIT Media Lab, this innovative company creates software that enables users to organize and navigate information from a variety of perspectives. Our client informed us that they needed a holiday greeting card with a whimsical message to offset the serious, technical nature of their software. We suggested that the project could also function as a promotional piece to be used at upcoming trade shows in the New Year. Through close collaboration, we decided that a flip book would be the ideal vehicle for demonstrating, on paper, an immersive Perspecta navigation experience. This format lent itself perfectly to a weekly calendar to usher in the New Year.
Nathan Durrant
Jennifer Tolo

Jeffrey Metzner

Companies and businesses big and small have been sending various forms of calendars out to their client base at the New Year as a form of promotion for many years. It is probably the most common form of self-promotion. From "girlie calendars" made by tire or carburetor companies and the little easel calendars made by banks to large scale art calendars made as promotion for photographers, artists, illustrators, and design companies, calendars have become an art form. Some calendars—such as Vargas, Currier & Ives, Marilyn Monroe, and Bette Grable—are famous. Everybody gets at least one calendar each year, and sometimes more than one. Because of the commonality of this form, it is surprising when someone actually approaches the design of a calendar from an entirely different and unique point of view. This is why I have chosen the calendar designed by Elixer Designs for Perspecta, Inc. as my Judge's Choice. This is the first time that I have ever seen a calendar that expresses the idea of the passing of a year in time and space. It's the only time that I have ever seen time move in calendar form. I have always been a lover of time-lapse photography and I have shot thousands of hours of time-lapse film over the years in different seasons in varied locations. Each film is always completely unique and reveals an aspect of life that I had never seen before. This little flip book expresses the year 1998 in time-lapse, and again and again something unexpected is revealed.

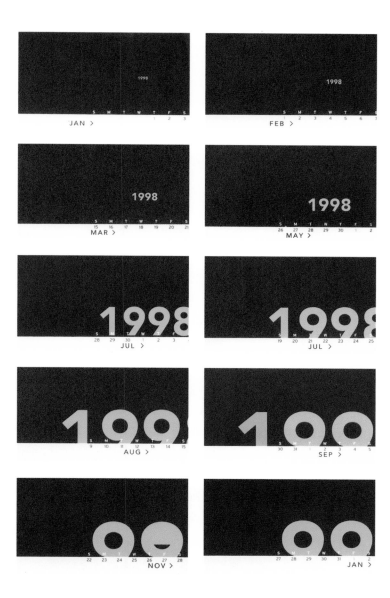

CALENDAR

Design
**Nathan Durrant
and Jennifer Tolo**
San Francisco, California

Art Direction
**Jennifer Jerde
and Lisa Strausfeld**

Studio
Elixir Design, Inc.

Client
Perspecta, Inc.

Principal Type
**Avenir and
Interstate**

Dimensions
**2 x 3¹/₂ in.
(5.1 x 8.9 cm)**

POSTER

DESIGN
Jennifer Sterling
San Francisco, California

LETTERING
Jennifer Sterling

ART DIRECTION
Jennifer Sterling

CREATIVE DIRECTION
Jennifer Sterling

COPYWRITER
Corey Weinstein

DESIGN OFFICE
Jennifer Sterling Design

CLIENT
**San Francisco
Performances**

PRINCIPAL TYPE
**Keedy, Garamond,
and handlettering**

DIMENSIONS
**48 x 68 in.
(121.9 x 172.7 cm)**

**Unanimous
Judges' Choice**

L. Richard Poulin

At the beginning of our two days of judging, I thought it would be more than difficult to choose one entry, out of approximately three thousand, for my Judge's Choice. At the end of the first day, it was almost impossible. Fortunately, the second day proved me wrong. When I entered the room where the posters were being displayed, I was immediately drawn to Jennifer Sterling's poster series. Their scale alone gave them an immediacy and presence that no other poster in the show possessed. Bold, raw letterforms and imagery drew me closer. Typographically and compositionally, they are pure theater—graphic elements moving across a stage through time and space, interacting with one another, performing, sparking my imagination, making the experience memorable. You want to connect with these posters, as well as with the performances they are all about. Here, typography is narrative, interpretive, and expressive. As I left the room, re-energized and inspired, I wished that I lived in San Francisco. If so, I would have been one of the first in line to purchase tickets for these performances.

What is your project called?
San Francisco Performances Posters
What is it?
A series of bus shelter posters designed for San Francisco Performances that announces upcoming performances by Anne Teresa de Keersmaeker/Rosas, Wim Vandekeybus/ Ultima Vez, DV8 Physical Theatre, Eiko and Koma with the Kronos Quartet, and the Stephen Petronio Company. The performances feature quite different elements of dance and the individual posters needed to reflect the works of these various dance companies. The companies had little or no photography to work with, so the typography became responsible for evoking the dance or experience of each performance.
Jennifer Sterling

Neil Powell

In this year's TDC show you will find many examples of typography which are, for whatever reason, more appealing than my Judge's Choice— "Auf Achse/Travelling." You will see type that is cooler. Type that catches your eye. Type as illustration. Type as decoration. Brochures and posters that use the latest Barry Deck fonts. They are great pieces, and I love most of them. But in "Auf Achse/Travelling," the viewer is taken on a trip-hop, computerized, synthetic, fictional journey through a make-believe country where type is relegated to its purest form— communication. Nuggets of information act as a tour guide as you are led on this visual excursion. A quote from the entrant explains "The country we visited is nonexistent: maps, money, language, public transport, filling stations, traffic signs, and supermarket junk—every item we present in our book is our own design." What a dream! Now, I don't know about you, but my temptation to go wild with type would have been uncontrollable. Every new application would have been a chance to outdesign the previous one. But here the designer has exercised remarkable restraint. A restraint which is the backbone of this piece. It is a complete world, and type acts as the gravitational field—pulling information, photography, and illustration together as a single, unified expression.

lahm Ausgabe Nr. 6: "Auf Achse/Travelling" reports a fictional journey in book form. The country we visited is nonexistent: maps, money, language, public transport, filling stations, traffic signs, and supermarket junk—every item we present in our book is our own design. Seemingly documentary-style still video frames of the countryside, cityscape, and interior views enhance the realism of our fictional journey; the black plastic cover, with its transparent holder for the (exchangeable) title, seeks to establish a formal affinity with that of commercially-available video-tapes. An invented local graphic designer with literary ambitions—Tim Frilander— provides detailed descriptions and ironic commentaries on the use of designer products of all kinds; and he assures us that even in this frequently innovative country people haven't yet ceased to struggle with the petty mishaps of daily life such as jammed lids of rubbish bins. The enclosed map enables the reader to exactly follow "lahm's" route around the country. Money is provided, too. But when packing your suitcase be warned: the weather is, more often than not, rather dismal.

Lutz Eberle
Andreas Jung
Marcus Wichmann

BOOK

DESIGN
**Lutz Eberle,
Andreas Jung, and
Marcus Wichmann**
Stuttgart, Germany

SCHOOL
**Staatliche Akademie
der Bildenden Künste**

PRINCIPAL TYPE
**Akzidenz Grotesk,
Bell Centennial,
lahm 6font,
and Mrs. Eaves**

DIMENSIONS
**9⅝ x 7⅛ in.
(24.5 x 18 cm)**

TDC44 Entries Selected for Typographic Excellence

Selected Entries

POSTER

DESIGN
Giorgio Pesce
Lausanne, Switzerland

LETTERING
Giorgio Pesce

ART DIRECTION
Giorgio Pesce

CREATIVE DIRECTION
Giorgio Pesce

AGENCY
Atelier Poisson

CLIENT
Festival de Théâtre Universitaire

PRINCIPAL TYPE
DIN, Meta, and handlettering

DIMENSIONS
$50^3/8$ x $35^5/8$ in. (128 x 90.5 cm)

BOOK

DESIGN
Paul Carlos
New York, New York

ART DIRECTION
**Paul Carlos and
J. Abbott Miller**

CREATIVE DIRECTION
J. Abbott Miller

DESIGN OFFICE
**Design/Writing/Research
New York**

CLIENT
**Davis Museum &
Cultural Center,
Wellesley College
and
Harry N. Abrams, Inc.**

PRINCIPAL TYPE
Quadraat and Whirligig

DIMENSIONS
**8⁷⁄₈ x 14¹⁄₄ in.
(22.5 x 36.2 cm)**

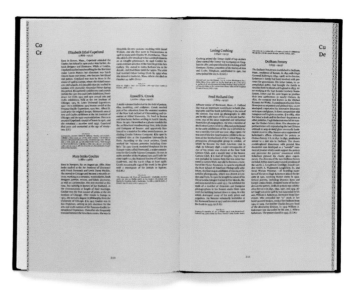

ANNUAL REPORT

DESIGN
Sharrie Brooks
San Francisco, California

ART DIRECTION
Bill Cahan

CREATIVE DIRECTION
Bill Cahan

DESIGN OFFICE
Cahan & Associates

CLIENT
Cell Genesys

PRINCIPAL TYPE
**News Gothic and
Adobe Caslon**

DIMENSIONS
**9$^{1}/_{2}$ x 11 in.
(24.1 x 27.9 cm)**

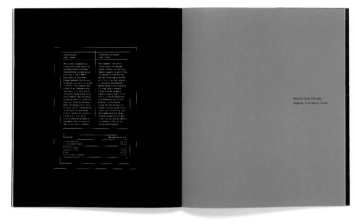

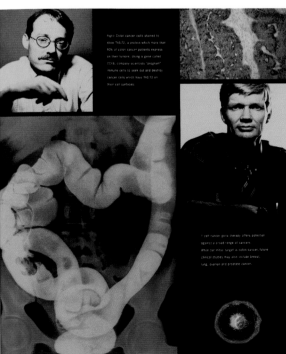

Phase I/II Clinical Testing

Oncology

T Cell Cancer Gene Therapy

In our lead cancer gene therapy program, Cell Genesys is engineering T cells which are harvested from the patient's blood via standard blood bank procedures. Utilizing a gene referred to as CC49, company scientists are modifying the T cells to recognize and bind to specific proteins found on certain types of cancer cells. Since a normal action of T cells is to destroy the specific target to which they bind, introduction of these engineered cells into the patient's body may potentially eliminate the existing cancer. Initial Phase I/II clinical studies at Stanford University and the University of California San Francisco will target advanced colon cancer. Future clinical studies may also include breast, lung, ovarian and prostate cancer.

Our product development pipeline includes several additional cancer gene therapies which target other specific proteins on cancer cells. Among them, T cell product candidates have already demonstrated specific killing of breast, ovarian and colon cancer cells in preclinical studies. Modified bone marrow stem cells also have shown anti-tumor activity in early preclinical studies. Our objective is to develop a number of highly targeted cancer gene therapies that specifically destroy the patient's tumor cells while leaving healthy cells unharmed. These gene therapies may prove particularly useful in treating patients whose immune systems have been impaired by radiation or chemotherapy.

Upper left: Alan Venook, M.D.,
University of California
San Francisco
Right: George Fisher, M.D.
Stanford University

14

ANNUAL REPORT

DESIGN
Bob Dinetz
San Francisco, California

CALLIGRAPHY
Bob Dinetz

ART DIRECTION
Bill Cahan

CREATIVE DIRECTION
Bill Cahan

DESIGN OFFICE
Cahan & Associates

CLIENT
Geron Corporation

PRINCIPAL TYPE
**Rosewood Fill,
Trade Gothic, and
handlettering**

DIMENSIONS
**Large book: 7¹⁄₂ x 11 in.
(19.1 x 27.9 cm)
Small book: 4⁵⁄₈ x 6 in.
(11.7 x 15.2 cm)**

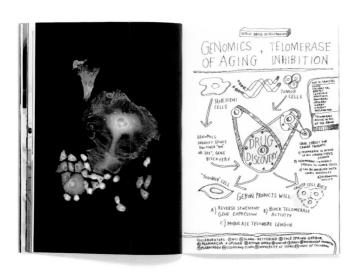

MORE WORK

1 An Identity Program

GENERAL ELECTRIC

AN ILLUSTRATED HISTORIC REVIEW

THE PROBLEM

Appearance vs. Reality. *Against the backdrop of vigorous corporate reorganization and streamlining, GE had remained a visual anachronism. Little had changed in the company's identity since 1890, when the now familiar GE Monogram was pressed into service shortly after the company's founding. While most major American companies had worked through the strategic design process to change or update corporate and brand identities at least once, GE stood apart, to a truncation of its visual heritage.*

The basic identity, the General Electric signature, worked against the company's marketing communicators. Their charge was to convey outside GE the revitalization spreading so rapidly inside, and they thought the GE identity contradicted their mandate. For them the long-standing signature failed to signal change of any sort, and instead suggested that GE was no different from the company it was in the 1920s or 1920s. But these communicators were in for a rude awakening.

GE's Manager of Corporate Identity, Merle Bonthuis, remembers, "We formed an Advisory Council. We asked a number of marketing communicators to bring examples of the communications they used in their business, everything from stationery, ads and brochures to signs and vehicles. When we put it all up on a wall and took a good look, we were quite surprised. We had expected to agree that the signature was old-fashioned and needed to be changed. But what we saw was a much bigger problem: an system anywhere, everybody 'doing their own thing.' Nothing looked coordinated and much of it looked dated. Overall, there was a feeling of inferior quality. With some embarrassment we realized we were part of the problem."

Ideas about *campaigns* surfaced in that initial meeting. A glance at business names revealed questionable practices. On each name were hung various organizational terms, as if the precise enunciation of the complex corporate bureaucracy was significant to GE's markets—an assumption the marketing communicators doubted. Fortified by their sense of discovery, this early group even questioned the accuracy of the corporate name. In view of Welch's tightly focused reorganization, was it correct to call the company "general?" With less than 20 percent of sales derived from electrical businesses, did "electric" make sense?

Armed with the disarray of this minimal visual audit plus a few ideas about naming, Richard Costello, GE's Manager of Corporate Marketing Communications, and Merle Bonthuis convinced senior management to hire a consultant in *corporate identity*.

Paul von Oelen, Executive Vice President, recalls, "We had no idea how poorly we were identifying our company. Jack Welch had turned the company around, but here we were, looking as though nothing had changed."

"Convincing management of the need to do something was not so difficult, but picking the consultant was," says Mr. Costello, especially since nobody in GE had ever worked with a corporate identity specialist.

"Our selection criteria featured design and process,

but they also evolved as we interviewed the candidates," says Mr. Bonthuis. "And we were hoping we could rely on a collective 'gut reaction' among the council members."

Mr. Costello adds, "In the final analysis, that *reaction* grew in importance but was tempered by knowledge we gained through the long review process. Design quality quickly became a most point since each of the consulting firms presented what we judged to be sound design."

"The only thing we ultimately thought we should push against was a specific 'look' or style that might characterize a consultant's design," says Mr. Bonthuis. "At that point, we didn't feel we could fairly evaluate the merits of any firm's look over that of another. So we chose a consultant who showed us a variety of designs without discernible common characteristics, hoping to keep our options open."

The strategic design process plus was not a point of differentiation among the consultants. "The process offered by all consultants is generally the same. But because management interviews play a key role in the first analytical phase, we began to put more emphasis on 'chemistry' as a criterion," says Mr. Bonthuis.

"We realized we had to look hard at how the consultant would talk to our people, how well he or she could participate in the GE culture," remarks Mr. Costello. "I remember the principal of another consultancy, who we thought would get along very easily with our people. But we later realized that he talked so much like GE people, we feared he would think just like us and fail to challenge us. Interesting how an initially positive evaluation turns negative as implications resolve.

"Finally, we placed our faith in a *consultant team* led by a fellow who had a kind of mischievous, renegade quality. To us that meant if we needed some really visionary thinking—the spark of real creativity—we had it on tap."

"The next criterion was internationality," says Mr. Bonthuis. "Because our markets are increasingly global and more of our visibility lies in international joint ventures and strategic alliances, it was critical to us that our identity consultant operate internationally and have first-hand experience in world markets."

"The other criteria were relatively minor considerations," concludes Mr. Costello. "We did consider the size and age of the project team. We tended to lean toward a large group of young people because we knew we would be working with the consultant for several years to come, and we wanted fresh thinking."

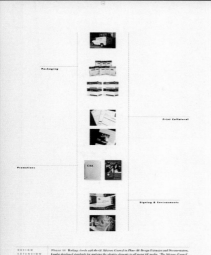

Packaging

Print Collateral

Promotions

Signing & Environments

DESIGN EXTENSION

Phase III: Working closely with the GE Advisory Council in Phase III: Design Extension and Documentation, Landor developed standards for applying the identity elements to all major GE media. The Advisory Council was absolutely critical to the successful next step of the program, recalls Mr. Bonthuis. *If only because through the council, the entire company participated consistently in developing the program. In Phase III the council broke up into small groups to help define not only the breadth of each media category, but also the practical limitations and requirements imposed by each kind of application. Although the Landor team had extensive experience in implementing programs, we wanted to be sure our specific needs were clearly defined.*

Once the Advisory Council subcommittees reviewed Landor's analysis and recommendations and granted their approval, the recommendations were deemed acceptable throughout the company.

Richard Costello says, "One of the smartest things we did was to ask several of our major advertising agencies to 'try out' the new graphic system almost as soon as management had approved it.

"We assembled seven of the agencies serving the major businesses, including our long-standing corporate agency, and Landor presented its 'working assumptions,' including use of a simple typeface, (DC New Baskerville, for all headlines and text. Then we asked the agencies to translate existing ads using the new graphic system

and to tell us what problems they encountered.

"Some of the agencies feared the worst and protested that the graphic signature, particularly the lower line, would take up too much space. One agency went so far as to prevent a statistical analysis comparing 'before' space to 'after' space, as if jamming every square inch full of something was the object of advertising.

"As you might guess, most agencies did a great job, showing how easily the graphic signature could fit into a well-designed layout. Some creative directors even made the point that the signature helped to structure the ads and keep them simple. They were right, and they won the day.

> "One of the smartest things we did was to ask several of our major advertising agencies to 'try out' the new graphic system almost as soon as management had approved it."

DESIGN
Cinthia Wen
San Francisco, California

CREATIVE DIRECTION
Nancy Hoefig

WRITER
Peter Allen

AGENCY
Landor Associates

CLIENT
General Electric

PRINCIPAL TYPE
Bodoni and Futura

DIMENSIONS
**8¼ x 11¾ in.
(21 x 29.9 cm)**

BROCHURE

Design
Jean-François Porchez
Malakoff, France

Lettering
Jean-François Porchez

Art Direction
Jean-François Porchez

Creative Direction
Jean-François Porchez

Studio
Porchez Typofonderie

Principal Type
Le Monde "Multistyle Family"

Dimensions
11⅝ x 16½ in. (29.7 x 42 cm)

PORCHEZ Typofonderie
www.porcheztypo.com
38 bis avenue Augustin-Dumont
F-92240 Malakoff, France
33 (0) 1 46 54 26 92
jfporchez@hol.fr

Tout sur le caractère Le Monde

Conçu en deux langues, ce spécimen évoque tous les aspects de la création : des influences jusqu'à la présentation de la famille au grand complet.

Le Monde

DIRECTEUR DE LA PUBLICATION : JEAN-FRANÇOIS PORCHEZ — SPÉCIMEN DU CARACTÈRE LE MONDE — UN CARACTÈRE EXCLUSIF CRÉÉ PAR JEAN-FRANÇOIS PORCHEZ

Parcourt
Lire neuf, grand & beau
A type family story

Echoing old style faces

La Totale typographie

MAGAZINE SPREAD

DESIGN
**Fred Woodward
and Gail Anderson**
New York, New York

LETTERING
Eric Siry

ART DIRECTION
Fred Woodward

CLIENT
Rolling Stone

PRINCIPAL TYPE
Fobia

DIMENSIONS
**12 x 20 in.
(30.5 x 50.8 cm)**

perry **ogden**

wickLow, kil-
dare. + dublin

25

march

Futurist design shirt with small soft collar over very full trousers with braces.

MAGAZINE SPREAD

DESIGN
David Carson
New York, New York

ART DIRECTION
David Carson

STUDIO
David Carson Design

CLIENT
Giorgio Armani

PRINCIPAL TYPE
Avenir

DIMENSIONS
**13 x 20 in.
(33 x 50.8 cm)**

MAGAZINE SPREAD

DESIGN
David Carson
New York, New York

ART DIRECTION
David Carson

STUDIO
David Carson Design

CLIENT
Giorgio Armani

PRINCIPAL TYPE
Avenir

DIMENSIONS
13 x 20 in.
(33 x 50.8 cm)

luis
sanchis
new york

march
31

Full trousers in light iridescent velvet, with
small, very tight jacket.

Chalk-stripe caban with patch pockets
and hidden zipper.

40

CATALOG

DESIGN
**Achim Heine,
Michael Lenz,
Peter Zizka, and
Sonia Reck**
Frankfurt, Germany

PHOTOGRAPHY
Tom Vack
Como, Italy

DESIGN STUDIO
Heine/Lenz/Zizka

CLIENT
**Nils Holger
Moormann**

PRINCIPAL TYPE
Franklin Gothic

DIMENSIONS
**$4\frac{1}{8}$ x $5\frac{7}{8}$ in.
(10.5 x 14.8 cm)**

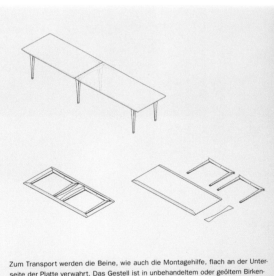

Zum Transport werden die Beine, wie auch die Montagehilfe, flach an der Unterseite der Platte verwahrt. Das Gestell ist in unbehandeltem oder geöltem Birkensperrholz erhältlich, die Tischplatte mit blauer, roter oder schwarzer Linoleumoberfläche sowie unbehandeltem Birkensperrholz oder mit lackiertem Birken-, Ahorn- oder Apfelfurnier.

: For storage and transport, the legs as well as the assembly tool fit into the underside of the tabletop. The frame is available in untreated or oiled birch plywood. The tabletop comes in a blue, red, or black linoleum surface as well as in untreated birch plywood or with lacquered birch, maple, or apple veneer.

/Jakob Gebert, 1996

spanoto

PROGRAM DESIGN
**Stacy Drummond
and Tracy Boychuk**
New York, New York

ART DIRECTION
**Jeffrey Keyton,
Stacy Drummond,
and Tracy Boychuk**

CREATIVE DIRECTION
**Jeffrey Keyton and
Stacy Drummond**

PHOTOGRAPHY
Jason Stang

AGENCY
**MTV: Video Music
Awards**

STUDIO
**MTV: Off-Air
Creative**

CLIENT
**MTV: Music
Television**

PRINCIPAL TYPE
Goudy

DIMENSIONS
**6¹/₄ x 9¹/₄ in.
(15.9 x 23.5 cm)**

ANNUAL REPORT

DESIGN
Jennifer Sterling
San Francisco, California

LETTERING
Jennifer Sterling

ART DIRECTION
Jennifer Sterling

COPYWRITER
Lisa Citron

DESIGN OFFICE
**Jennifer Sterling
Design**

CLIENT
**Blue Shield of
California**

PRINCIPAL TYPE
Garamond and Meta

DIMENSIONS
**6¼ x 10¼ in.
(15.9 x 26 cm)**

DESIGN
Imboden Melchior
Buochs, Switzerland

ART DIRECTION
Imboden Melchior

CREATIVE DIRECTION
Imboden Melchior

DESIGN OFFICE
Design Office
Imboden Melchior

POSTER

DESIGN
Wang Xu
Guangzhou, China

ART DIRECTION
Wang Xu

CREATIVE DIRECTION
Wang Xu

STUDIO
**Wang Xu &
Associates Ltd.**

CLIENT
China Youth Press

PRINCIPAL TYPE
Myriamm

DIMENSIONS
**34⅝ x 24¹³⁄₁₆ in.
(88 x 63 cm)**

the New Edition
of Design Exchange
no.12

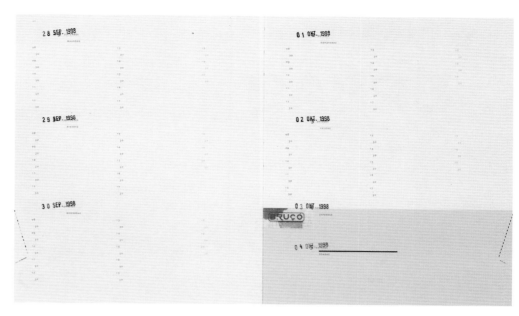

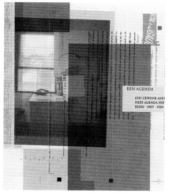

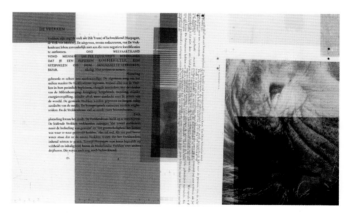

CALENDAR

DESIGN
Bau Winkel
The Hague, Netherlands

ART DIRECTION
Bau Winkel

CREATIVE DIRECTION
Bau Winkel

STUDIO
Studio Bau Winkel

CLIENT
Ando

PRINCIPAL TYPE
Frutiger, Bembo, Thesis, and Trinité

DIMENSIONS
**8³⁄₈ x 9⁵⁄₈ in.
(21.2 x 24.5 cm)**

48

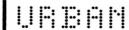

LOGOTYPE

DESIGN
**Howard Brown,
Mike Calkins, and
Lance Rusoff**
Philadelphia, Pennsylvania

ART DIRECTION
Howard Brown

AGENCY
Urban Outfitters

PRINCIPAL TYPE
Various

POSTER

DESIGN
Kevin Brainard
New York, New York

ART DIRECTION
Drew Hodges

DESIGN OFFICE
Spot Design

CLIENT
Maxine Taupin

PRINCIPAL TYPE
**Franklin Gothic
and Champion**

DIMENSIONS
**24 x 36 in.
(61 x 91.4 cm)**

TRAILER

DESIGN
Inka Kardys and
Matthias Zentner
Munich, Germany

ART DIRECTION
Inka Kardys and
Matthias Zentner

CREATIVE DIRECTION
Inka Kardys and
Matthias Zentner

EDITOR
Jochen Kraus

COPYWRITER
Michael Conford

DESIGN STUDIO
Velvet Mediendesign

CLIENT
VOX Television

PRINCIPAL TYPE
Muff and handlettering

PACKAGING

DESIGN
**Clifford Stoltze and
Robert Beerman**
Boston, Massachusetts

ART DIRECTION
**Clifford Stoltze and
Robert Beerman**

STUDIO
Stoltze Design

CLIENT
Matador Records

PRINCIPAL TYPE
**Zapf Dingbats, Vitrina,
Flightcase, Big Ed-Sr.,
and Info**

DIMENSIONS
**12 x 12 in.
(30.5 x 30.5 cm)**

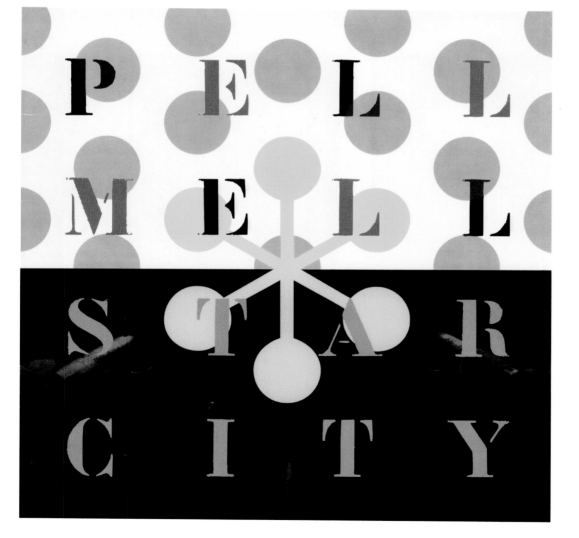

PROMOTION

DESIGN
Jason Eplawy
Chicago, Illinois

ART DIRECTION
Mary Moegenburg

CREATIVE DIRECTION
Dana Arnett

DESIGN OFFICE
VSA Partners, Inc.

CLIENT
Potlatch Corporation

PRINCIPAL TYPE
Cooper Black and Univers

DIMENSIONS
7¼ x 9¾ in. (18.4 x 24.8 cm)

PROGRAM

DESIGN
Giorgio Pesce
Lausanne, Switzerland

LETTERING
Giorgio Pesce

ART DIRECTION
Giorgio Pesce

CREATIVE DIRECTION
Giorgio Pesce

AGENCY
Atelier Poisson

CLIENT
Théâtre Arsenic

PRINCIPAL TYPE
**Triumvirate and
Trade Gothic**

DIMENSIONS
**7⁷⁄₈ x 1³⁄₈ in.
(20 x 3.5 cm)**

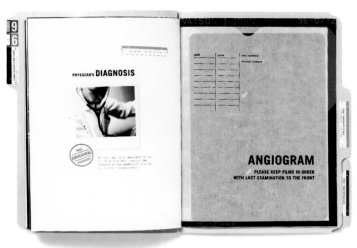

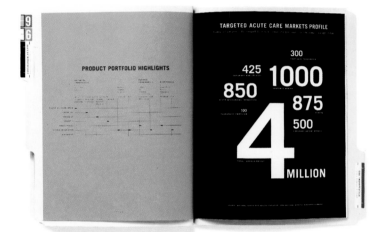

ANNUAL REPORT

DESIGN
Kevin Roberson
San Francisco, California

ART DIRECTION
Bill Cahan

CREATIVE DIRECTION
Bill Cahan

DESIGN OFFICE
Cahan & Associates

CLIENT
COR Therapeutics

PRINCIPAL TYPE
**Trade Gothic, Courier,
and Orator**

DIMENSIONS
**9¹⁄₂ x 11³⁄₄ in.
(24.1 x 29.9 cm)**

STATIONERY

DESIGN
Fritz Klaetke
Boston, Massachusetts

LETTERING
Fritz Klaetke

ART DIRECTION
Fritz Klaetke

CREATIVE DIRECTION
Fritz Klaetke

DESIGN OFFICE
Visual Dialogue

PRINCIPAL TYPE
News Halftone

DIMENSIONS
**7 x 9¹⁄₂ in.
(17.8 x 24.1 cm)**

CAMPAIGN

DESIGN
Chad Hagen
Minneapolis, Minnesota

CREATIVE DIRECTION
Bill Thorburn

PHOTOGRAPHY
Bill Phelps

COPYWRITER
Jonathan Sunshine

STUDIO
Carmichael Lynch Thorburn

CLIENT
Association of Children's Health Care-Minneapolis

PRINCIPAL TYPE
Trade Gothic

DIMENSIONS
Various

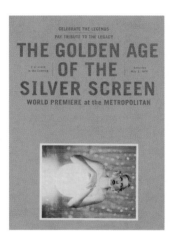

Design
Giorgio Pesce
Lausanne, Switzerland

Lettering
Giorgio Pesce

Art Direction
Giorgio Pesce

Creative Direction
Giorgio Pesce

Agency
Atelier Poisson

Client
Théâtre Arsenic

Principal Type
**ITC Officina and
handlettering**

Dimensions
**$7^7/_8$ x $12^9/_{16}$ in.
(20 x 32 cm)**

BOOK AND POSTER

DESIGN
**Joseph Becker
and Pascal Béjean**
Ann Arbor, Michigan and
Paris, France

LETTERING
**Joseph Becker
and Pascal Béjean**

ART DIRECTION
**Joseph Becker
and Pascal Béjean**

CREATIVE DIRECTION
**Joseph Becker
and Pascal Béjean**

PHOTOGRAPHY
**Joseph Becker
and Pascal Béjean**

PUBLISHER
**Bleu Élastique and
Bulldozer® Éditions**

PRINCIPAL TYPE
Random Access

DIMENSIONS
**Book: 3 x 7⁷/₈ in.
(7.5 x 20 cm)
Poster: 27¹/₂ x 40¹/₈ in.
(70 x 102 cm)**

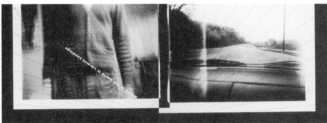

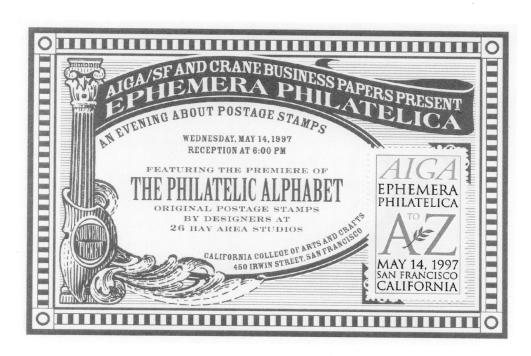

CAMPAIGN

DESIGN
**Michael Osborne
and Paul Kagiwada**
San Francisco, California

CREATIVE DIRECTION
Michael Osborne

STUDIO
**Michael Osborne
Design**

CLIENT
**American Institute
of Graphic Arts**

PRINCIPAL TYPE
Centaur

DIMENSIONS
**3³/₁₆ x 5³/₄ in.
(9.7 x 14.6 cm)**

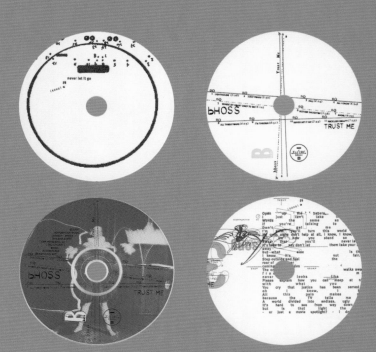

PACKAGING

DESIGN
Jennifer Sterling
San Francisco, California

LETTERING
Jennifer Sterling

ART DIRECTION
Jennifer Sterling

COPYWRITER
Deonne Kahler

DESIGN OFFICE
Jennifer Sterling Design

CLIENT
Bhoss

PRINCIPAL TYPE
**Garamond, Meta,
Helvetica, and Keedy**

DIMENSIONS
**4¼ x 4¼ in.
(10.8 x 10.8 cm)**

STATIONERY

DESIGN
**Annetta Sappenfield
and Ron Anderson**
New York, New York

ART DIRECTION
John Parham

CREATIVE DIRECTION
Maruchi Santana

AGENCY
Parham Santana, Inc.

PRINCIPAL TYPE
Interstate and Univers

DIMENSIONS
**8½ x 11 in.
(21.6 x 27.9 cm)**

PARHAM | SANTANA

PARHAM | SANTANA
7 West 18th Street New York, New York 10011

7 West 18th Street New York, New York 10011
T 212.645.7501 • F 212.645.8314

PARHAM | SANTANA

John Parham
President

7 West 18th Street New York, New York 10011
T 212.645.7501 • F 212.645.8314 • E-mail jparham@parhamsantana.com

BROCHURE

DESIGN
Charles Wilkin
Columbus, Ohio

ART DIRECTION
Charles Wilkin

STUDIO
**Automatic Art and
Design**

PRINCIPAL TYPE
**Folio Bold and Folio
Bold Condensed**

DIMENSIONS
**5½ x 5¾ in.
(14 x 14.6 cm)**

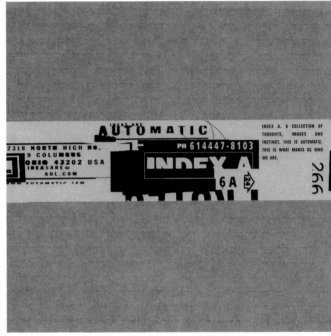

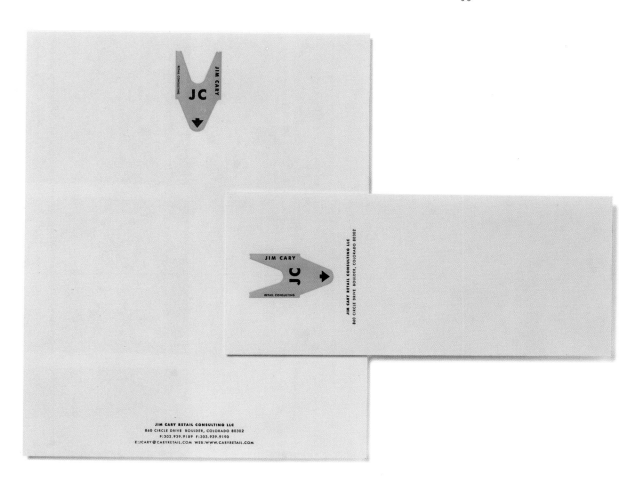

STATIONERY

DESIGN
Alisa Wolfson
Chicago, Illinois

ART DIRECTION
James Koval

DESIGN OFFICE
VSA Partners, Inc.

CLIENT
**Jim Cary Retail
Consulting**

PRINCIPAL TYPE
Futura

DIMENSIONS
**8¹⁄₂ x 11 in.
(21.6 x 27.9 cm)**

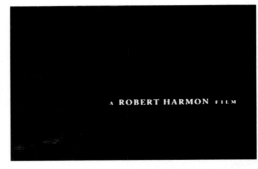

MAIN TITLES

DESIGN
**Garson Yu,
Kyle Cooper, and
Olivia D'Albis**
Hollywood, California

ART DIRECTION
Garson Yu

CREATIVE DIRECTION
Kyle Cooper

STUDIO
Imaginary Forces

CLIENT
HBO

PRINCIPAL TYPE
Sta Portable

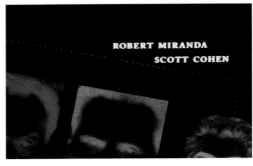

POSTER

Design
Dirk Wolfersdorf
Düsseldorf, Germany

Assistance
Helfried Hagenberg

Design Office
Wolfersdorf Design

Client
**Initiative für
Gewaltlosigkeit**

Principal Type
Franklin Gothic

Dimensions
**33¹⁄₈ x 23³⁄₈ in.
(84 x 59.4 cm)**

BOOK

DESIGN
Kipling Phillips
Hamburg, Germany

LETTERING
Kipling Phillips

ART DIRECTION
Kipling Phillips

CREATIVE DIRECTION
**Olaf Oldigs and
Thomas Walmrath**

SHARP SHOOTER
André Kemper

AGENCY
Springer & Jacoby

PRINCIPAL TYPE
**AG Stencil and
ITC Officina Sans**

DIMENSIONS
**8¼ x 5⅞ in.
(21 x 15 cm)**

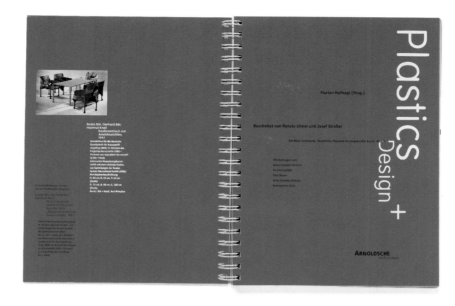

B O O K

Design
Silke Nalbach
Stuttgart, Germany

Art Direction
Silke Nalbach

Creative Direction
Silke Nalbach

Design Studio
**Silke Nalbach,
Typografik**

Client
**Arnoldsche Art
Publishers**

Principal Type
**ITC Officina Sans,
ITC Officina Serif,
and VAG Rounded**

Dimensions
**8⅝ x 11⅝ in.
(22 x 29.5 cm)**

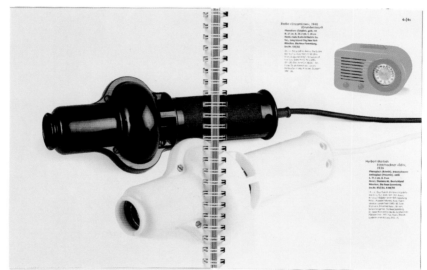

BOOK

DESIGN
Jason Eplawy
Chicago, Illinois

ART DIRECTION
Mary Moegenburg

CREATIVE DIRECTION
Dana Arnett

AGENCY
VSA Partners, Inc.

CLIENT
Potlatch Corporation

PRINCIPAL TYPE
**Bulmer, Janson,
Helvetica Rounded,
Franklin Gothic,
and Clarendon**

DIMENSIONS
**4¹⁄₈ x 5¹⁄₂ in.
(10.5 x 14 cm)**

In an age of digital boundary-pushing, energizing art to new frontiers, there is Myrtle Stedman. Aged, diminutive, graceful, she stands terra firma in unadorned contrast. Her world springs with the same organic purity that distinguishes the traditional New Mexico adobe architecture she helped champion.

She is a painter, a writer, and an architect with artistic appetites as expansive as a New Mexico sky. At 20 she married "an education," an accomplished artist, who inspired and challenged her to step out of his shadow to cast her own bright light. For Myrtle, art and life are one seamless adventure to unearth the mysteries of the creative mind. "I am so crazy to understand how the mind works. It just fills me all the time with the things I want to say and do."

It is a comfort and gift that Myrtle Stedman lives tucked snugly in the New Mexico mountains of Tusuque, living in the adobe home she built with her own hands. She rises before dawn daily filled with the rapture to create anew. At 89, she is both innocence and heirloom.

Down the bleak and ravaged stretch of road that lies smack in the middle of gritty, ghoulish Gary, Indiana, "murder capital of the world," there is the Badlands. Lording over it is the maestro of the unrefined. Swallow him whole. Make no mistake. There is no other Roy Boy.

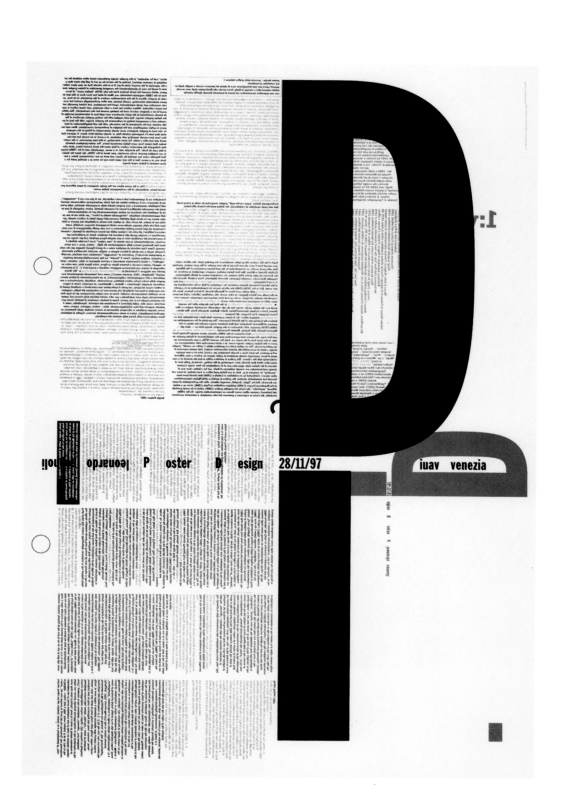

POSTER

DESIGN
Leonardo Sonnoli
Rimini, Italy

ART DIRECTION
Leonardo Sonnoli

CREATIVE DIRECTION
Leonardo Sonnoli

STUDIO
LS Design

PRINCIPAL TYPE
ITC Franklin

DIMENSIONS
**26³/₄ x 38⁹/₁₆ in.
(68 x 98 cm)**

Thomas Mann als Inspiration

Ein künstlerisches Projekt in der Thomas-Mann-Straße

4. bis 11. Oktober 1996

Informationen: Kunst Forum Bonn, Thomas-Mann-Straße 36   0228. 63 39 58

POSTER

DESIGN
Heribert Birnbach
Bonn, Germany

ART DIRECTION
Heribert Birnbach

CREATIVE DIRECTION
Heribert Birnbach

STUDIO
**Birnbach Design,
Studio für
Konzeption und
visuelle Gestaltung**

CLIENT
Kunst Forum Bonn

PRINCIPAL TYPE
**Interstate, DIN,
and Frutiger**

DIMENSIONS
**23³/₈ x 33¹/₈ in.
(59.4 x 84.1 cm)**

BOOK

DESIGN
**Fons M. Hickmann
and Ulysses Voelker**
Düsseldorf, Germany

ART DIRECTION
**Ulysses Voelker and
Fons M. Hickmann**

PHOTOGRAPHY
Dieter Leistner
Mainz, Germany

STUDIO
Fons M. Hickmann

CLIENT
**Busse & Geitner
Architects and
H. M. Nelte Verlag**

PRINCIPAL TYPE
Univers

DIMENSIONS
**9⁵⁄₈ x 12⁷⁄₁₆ in.
(24.5 x 31.5 cm)**

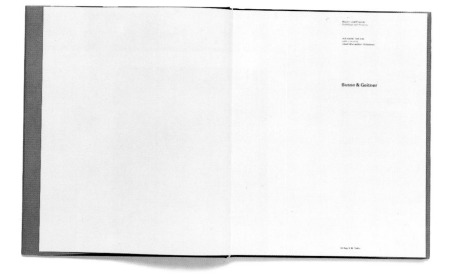

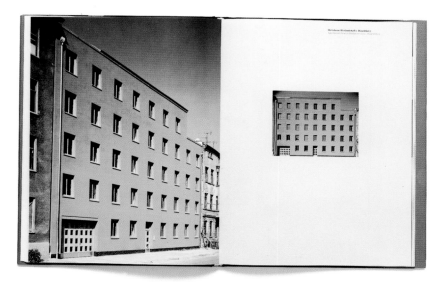

BOOK

DESIGN
**Eric Neuner
and Agatha Sohn**
New York, New York

STUDIO
E&A Design, Inc.

CLIENT
**Jordan Crandall,
X-Art Foundation,
and "Suspension"**

PRINCIPAL TYPE
Various

DIMENSIONS
**6¹¹⁄₁₆ x 9¹⁄₁₆ in.
(17 x 23 cm)**

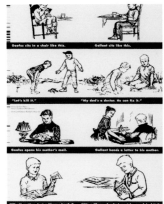

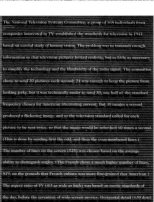

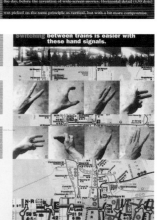

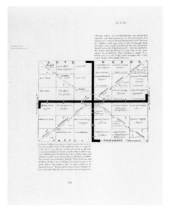

DESIGN
Lyne Lefebvre
Montreal, Quebec, Canada

ART DIRECTION
Lyne Lefebvre

CREATIVE DIRECTION
Bradford Gorman

AGENCY
**Behaviour
Design, Inc.**

CLIENT
Lux Films

POSTER AND PROGRAM

DESIGN
Giorgio Pesce
Lausanne, Switzerland

LETTERING
Giorgio Pesce

ART DIRECTION
Giorgio Pesce

CREATIVE DIRECTION
Giorgio Pesce

AGENCY
Atelier Poisson

CLIENT
**Les Urbaines-
festival de jeunes
créateurs**

PRINCIPAL TYPE
OCR and Digital

DIMENSIONS
**Poster: 50³/₈ x 35⁵/₈ in.
(128 x 90.5 cm)
Program: 5¹/₂ x 3¹/₂ in.
(14 x 9 cm)**

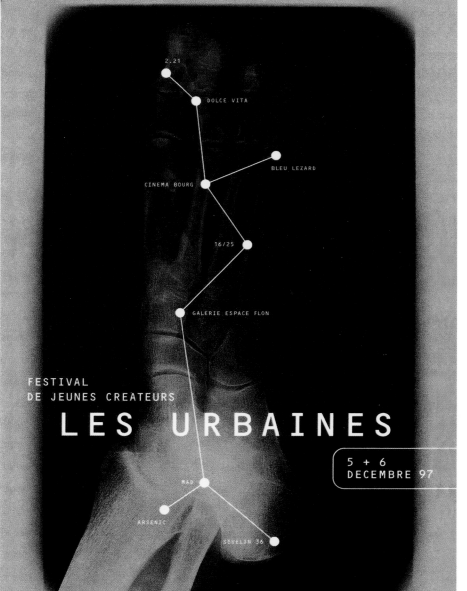

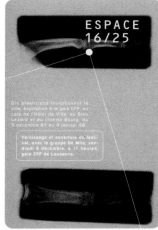

fondazione **don Gaudiano**

in collaborazione con
**Fondazione Cassa
di Risparmio di Pesaro**

Giancarlo Gaeta
Cultura dei Diritti
e Obbligo verso la città

Pesaro, 16 maggio 1997
Palazzo Montani Antaldi
piazza Antaldi, ore 18.00

dirittidoveri

POSTER DESIGN
Leonardo Sonnoli
Rimini, Italy
ART DIRECTION
Leonardo Sonnoli
CREATIVE DIRECTION
Leonardo Sonnoli
AGENCY
Dolcini associati
CLIENT
**Don Gaudiano
Foundation**
PRINCIPAL TYPE
ITC Officina
DIMENSIONS
**26³⁄₄ x 38⁹⁄₁₆ in.
(68 x 98 cm)**

ES

DESIGN
**Kyle Cooper,
Kurt Mattila,
Olivia D'Albis,
Adam Bluming,
and
Geoff Kaplan**
Hollywood, California

CREATIVE DIRECTION
Kyle Cooper

EDITOR
Kurt Mattila

STUDIO
Imaginary Forces

CLIENT
**Mandalay
Entertainment**

PRINCIPAL TYPE
Bell Gothic

DONNIE BRASCO

PRODUCTION DESIGNED BY
DONALD GRAHAM BURT

2   KODAK 5063

DIRECTOR OF PHOTOGRAPHY
PETER SOVA

DIRECTED BY MIKE NEWELL

ANNUAL REPORT

DESIGN
Bob Dinetz
San Francisco, California

ART DIRECTION
Bill Cahan

CREATIVE DIRECTION
Bill Cahan

DESIGN OFFICE
Cahan & Associates

CLIENT
**Cadence Design
Systems**

PRINCIPAL TYPE
**Trade Gothic and
Bembo**

DIMENSIONS
**8⁷/₈ x 11⁷/₈ in.
(22.5 x 30.2 cm)**

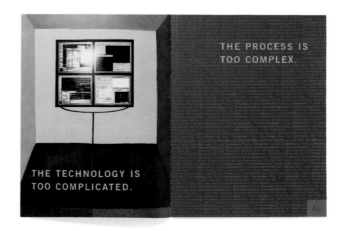

MAGAZINE SPREAD

DESIGN
David Carson
New York, New York

ART DIRECTION
David Carson

STUDIO
David Carson Design

CLIENT
Giorgio Armani

PRINCIPAL TYPE
Avenir

DIMENSIONS
13 x 20 in.
(33 x 50.8 cm)

Suit with one button jacket. White shirt with dark tie.

dah
Len
newYork
l
april

58
59

ANNUAL REPORT

DESIGN
Kevin Roberson
San Francisco, California

ART DIRECTION
Bill Cahan

CREATIVE DIRECTION
Bill Cahan

DESIGN OFFICE
Cahan & Associates

CLIENT
Xilinx, Inc.

PRINCIPAL TYPE
**Caslon and various
found letters**

DIMENSIONS
**6⁷⁄₈ x 8⁷⁄₈ in.
(17.5 x 22.5 cm)**

STATIONERY

DESIGN
Martha Graettinger
Madison, Wisconsin

ART DIRECTION
**Kevin Wade
and Dana Lytle**

CREATIVE DIRECTION
**Kevin Wade
and Dana Lytle**

DESIGN OFFICE
**Planet Design
Company**

PRINCIPAL TYPE
Nobel Family

DIMENSIONS
**8½ x 11 in.
(21.6 x 27.9 cm)**

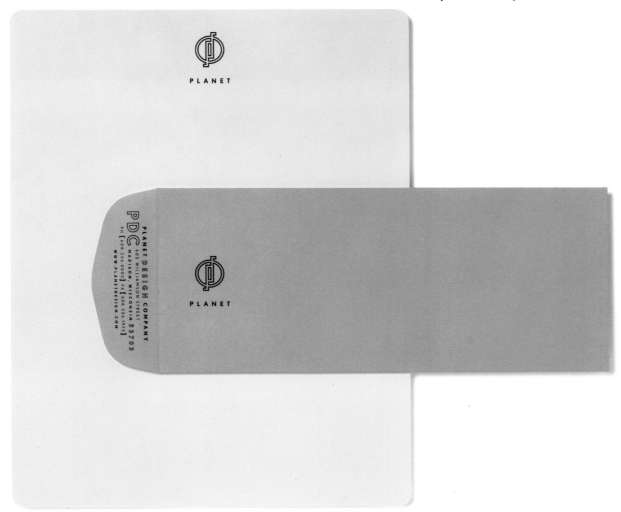

ANNUAL REPORT

DESIGN
**Joyce Nesnadny
and Michelle Moehler**
Cleveland, Ohio

ART DIRECTION
**Mark Schwartz
and Joyce Nesnadny**

CREATIVE DIRECTION
**Mark Schwartz
and Joyce Nesnadny**

PRINTER
Fortran Printing, Inc.

STUDIO
Nesnadny + Schwartz

CLIENT
**The Progressive
Corporation**

PRINCIPAL TYPE
News Gothic

DIMENSIONS
**8¹⁄₂ x 11 in.
(21.6 x 27.9 cm)**

ANNUAL REPORT

Design
Todd Simmons
Atlanta, Georgia

Creative Direction
Phil Hamlett

Photography
Andrew Bordwin
New York, New York

Studio
EAI

Client
Seagate Technology

Principal Type
DIN and Filosophia

Dimensions
**7¹⁄₂ x 10¹⁄₄ in.
(19.1 x 26 cm)**

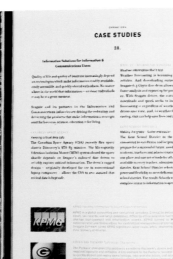

POSTER

DESIGN
Heribert Birnbach
Bonn, Germany

ART DIRECTION
Heribert Birnbach

CREATIVE DIRECTION
Heribert Birnbach

AGENCY
**Birnbach Design,
Studio für Konzeption
und visuelle Gestaltung**

CLIENT
Universität Wuppertal

PRINCIPAL TYPE
**Bureau, DIN, and
Franklin Gothic**

DIMENSIONS
**$61^{13}/_{16}$ x $73^{5}/_{8}$ in.
(157 x 187 cm)**

WEB SITE

DESIGN
Charles Wilkin
Columbus, Ohio

ART DIRECTION
Charles Wilkin

ILLUSTRATION
Charles Wilkin

STUDIO
**Automatic Art and
Design**

CLIENT
**Prototype Experimental
Foundry**

PRINCIPAL TYPE
**Superchunk, Nude,
and Ghetto Prince**

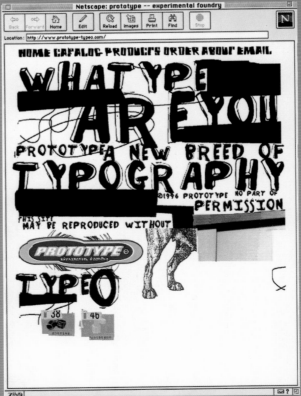

Lesson 1.

Literacy First

POSTER DESIGN
**Haley Johnson
and Richard Boynton**
Minneapolis, Minnesota

ART DIRECTION
Haley Johnson

STUDIO
**Haley Johnson
Design Company**

CLIENT
**American Institute of
Graphic Arts/Colorado**

PRINCIPAL TYPE
**Futura and Remington
typewriter type circa
1950**

DIMENSIONS
**24 x 36 in.
(61 x 91.4 cm)**

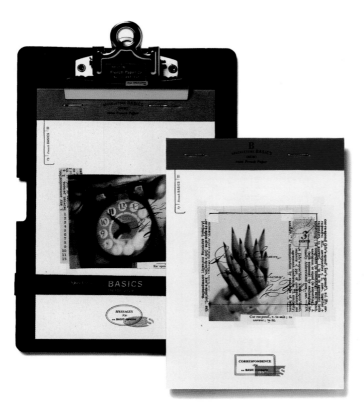

DIRECT MAIL

DESIGN
Laurie DeMartino
Minneapolis, Minnesota

ART DIRECTION
Laurie DeMartino

PHOTOGRAPHY
Steve Belkowitz
Philadelphia, Pennsylvania

COPYWRITER
Lisa Pemrick
Minneapolis, Minnesota

STUDIO
Studio d Design

CLIENT
French Paper Company

PRINCIPAL TYPE
**New Baskerville and
News Gothic**

DIMENSIONS
**5¹⁄₂ x 8¹⁄₂ in.
(14 x 21.6 cm)**

BOOK

DESIGN
**James Koval
and Steven Ryan**
Chicago, Illinois

ART DIRECTION
James Koval

CREATIVE DIRECTION
James Koval

AGENCY
VSA Partners, Inc.

CLIENT
**Mohawk Paper
Mills, Inc.**

PRINCIPAL TYPE
Various

DIMENSIONS
**12 x 7 in.
(30.5 x 17.8 cm)**

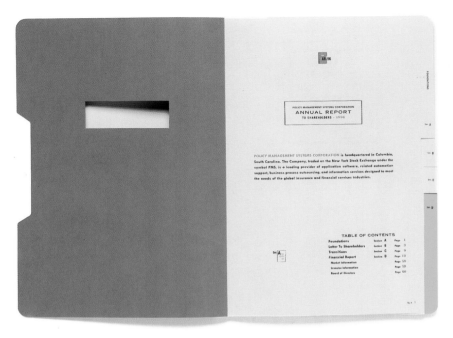

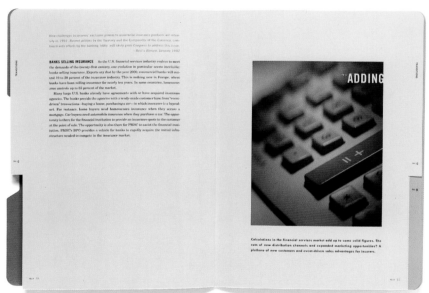

ANNUAL REPORT

DESIGN
Barry Townsend
Columbia, South Carolina

ART DIRECTION
Barry Townsend

CREATIVE DIRECTION
Barry Townsend

PHOTOGRAPHY
George Fulton

CLIENT
PMSC

PRINCIPAL TYPE
**Twentieth Century,
Trade Gothic,
and New Century
Schoolbook**

DIMENSIONS
**8 x 11 in.
(20.3 x 27.9 cm)**

STATIONERY

DESIGN
Peter Felder
Rankweil, Austria

LETTERING
Peter Felder

PRINTER
Wenin OHG
Dornbirn, Austria

DESIGN OFFICE
Felder Grafikdesign

PRINCIPAL TYPE
Univers

DIMENSIONS
8¼ x 11¹¹/₁₆ in.
(21 x 29.7 cm)

Unanimous
Judges'
Choice

MAGAZINE SPREAD

DESIGN
David Carson
New York, New York

ART DIRECTION
David Carson

STUDIO
David Carson Design

CLIENT
Giorgio Armani

PRINCIPAL TYPE
Avenir

DIMENSIONS
13 x 20 in.
(33 x 50.8 cm)

roxanne

low

emporio armani. madison avenue,

new york

-it

april
14

Clinging jersey with op-effect yoke.

89

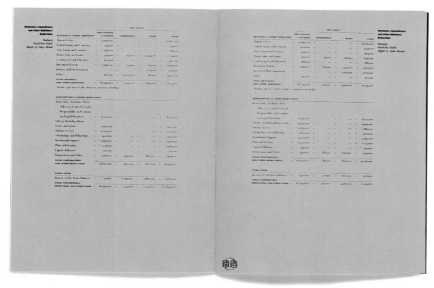

ANNUAL REPORT

DESIGN
**Mark Geer
and Karen Malnar**
Houston, Texas

ART DIRECTION
Mark Geer

STUDIO
Geer Design, Inc.

CLIENT
**South Texas
College of Law**

PRINCIPAL TYPE
**Centaur, Chicago,
and Monaco**

DIMENSIONS
**8 x 10¹/₂ in.
(20.3 x 26.7 cm)**

POSTER

DESIGN
Shuichi Nogami
Osaka, Japan

ART DIRECTION
Shuichi Nogami

DESIGN OFFICE
Nogami Design Office

CLIENT
Musa Co., Ltd.

PRINCIPAL TYPE
**Gadzooks Regular
and Univers Regular**

DIMENSIONS
**40½ x 28⅝ in.
(103 x 72.8 cm)**

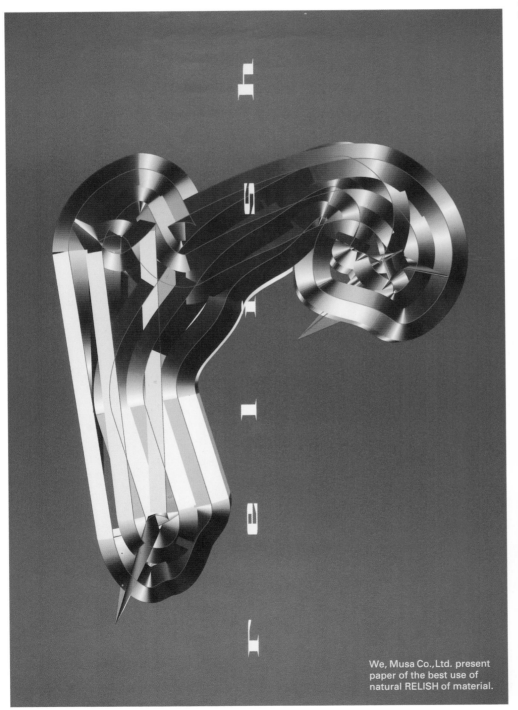

We, Musa Co.,Ltd. present paper of the best use of natural RELISH of material.

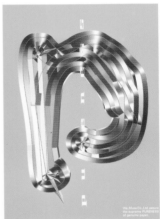

BROCHURE

DESIGN
Jennifer Sterling
San Francisco, California

LETTERING
Jennifer Sterling

ART DIRECTION
Jennifer Sterling

PHOTOGRAPHY
**John Casado,
Dave Magnusson,
Tony Stromberg,
and Marko Lavrisha**

DESIGN OFFICE
Jennifer Sterling Design

PRINCIPAL TYPE
**Garamond, Meta,
Orator, and
handlettering**

DIMENSIONS
**5¹⁄₂ x 7¹⁄₂ in.
(14 x 19.1 cm)**

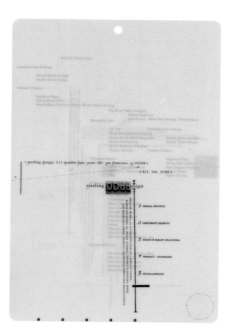

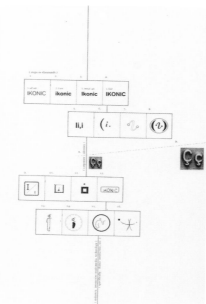

STATIONERY

DESIGN
John Bielenberg
San Francisco, California

STUDIO
Bielenberg Design

PRINCIPAL TYPE
Bell Gothic

DIMENSIONS
**8½ x 11 in.
(21.6 x 27.9 cm)**

**Unanimous
Judges' Choice**

BIELENBERG*

BIELENBERG DESIGN 245 FIFTH STREET #201 SAN FRANCISCO, CALIFORNIA 94103

BIELENBERG*

BIELENBERG DESIGN 245 FIFTH STREET #201 SAN FRANCISCO, CALIFORNIA 94103 TEL [415] 495-3371 FAX [415] 495-4842 EMAIL INFO@BIELENBERG.COM

BIELENBERG*

SEVA DYAKOV
BIELENBERG DESIGN 245 FIFTH ST. #201 SAN FRANCISCO, CA 94103
TEL [415] 495-3371 FAX [415] 495-4842 SEVA@BIELENBERG.COM

DESIGN
Bob Dinetz
San Francisco, California

ART DIRECTION
Bill Cahan

CREATIVE DIRECTION
Bill Cahan

DESIGN OFFICE
Cahan & Associates

CLIENT
Trek Bicycles

PRINCIPAL TYPE
Bembo

DIMENSIONS
**10 x 15½ in.
(25.4 x 39.4 cm)**

SOLUTIONS AREN'T BOUGHT

THEY'RE CREATED

IT LOOKS LIKE AEROSPACE TECHNOLOGY

BECAUSE IT IS.

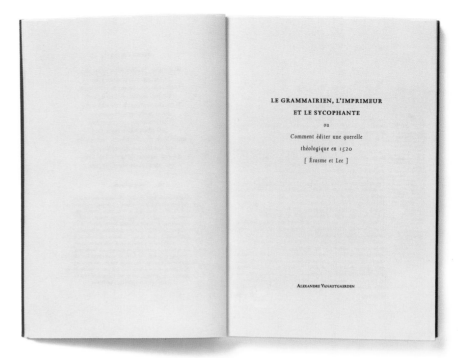

BOOK DESIGN
**Joël Van Audenhaege,
Franck Sarfati,
Olivier Sténuit, and
Raf Thienpont**
Brussels, Belgium

ART DIRECTION
**Joël Van Audenhaege,
Franck Sarfati,
and Olivier Sténuit**

AGENCY
[sign*]–Brussels

CLIENT
**La Maison
d'Erasme-Anderlecht**

PRINCIPAL TYPE
Joanna

DIMENSIONS
**5¹⁄₈ x 7¹⁄₂ in.
(13 x 19 cm)**

ANNUAL REPORT

DESIGN
**Peter Felder
and Renè Dalpra**
Rankweil, Austria

LETTERING
**Renè Dalpra
and Peter Felder**

ART DIRECTION
Peter Felder

PRINTER
Wenin OHG
Dornbirn, Austria

DESIGN OFFICE
Felder Grafikdesign

CLIENT
**Telefonseelsorge
Vorarlberg**

PRINCIPAL TYPE
Avenir Heavy

DIMENSIONS
**6^{11}/$_{16}$ x 9^{1}/$_{4}$ in.
(17 x 23.5 cm)**

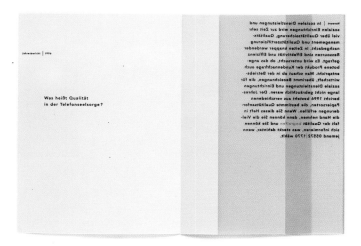

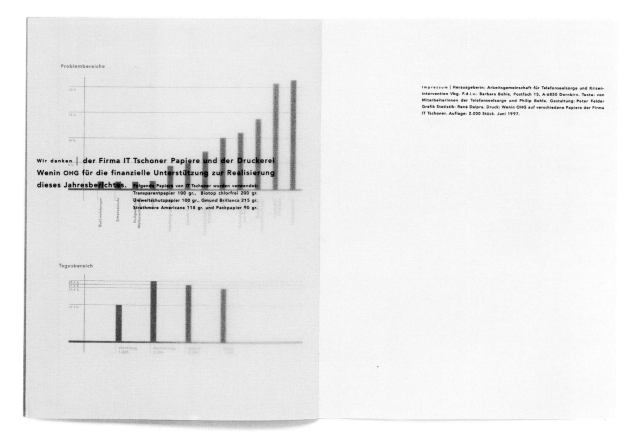

BOOK   DESIGN
Regine Thienhaus
Hamburg, Germany

STUDIO
**Trendbüro Peter
Wippermann und
Büro Hamburg**

CLIENT
**Verlag Hermann
Schmidt Mainz**

PRINCIPAL TYPE
Rotation and SpSans

DIMENSIONS
**7⅝ x 9¼ in.
(19.5 x 23.5 cm)**

POSTER

DESIGN
Ralph Schraivogel
Zurich, Switzerland

ART DIRECTION
Ralph Schraivogel

CREATIVE DIRECTION
Ralph Schraivogel

PHOTOGRAPHY
Peter Hunkeler

STUDIO
Schraivogel Design

CLIENT
**Zurich Museum
of Design**

PRINCIPAL TYPE
Metal stencil letters

DIMENSIONS
**35⅝ x 50⅜ in.
(90.5 x 128 cm)**

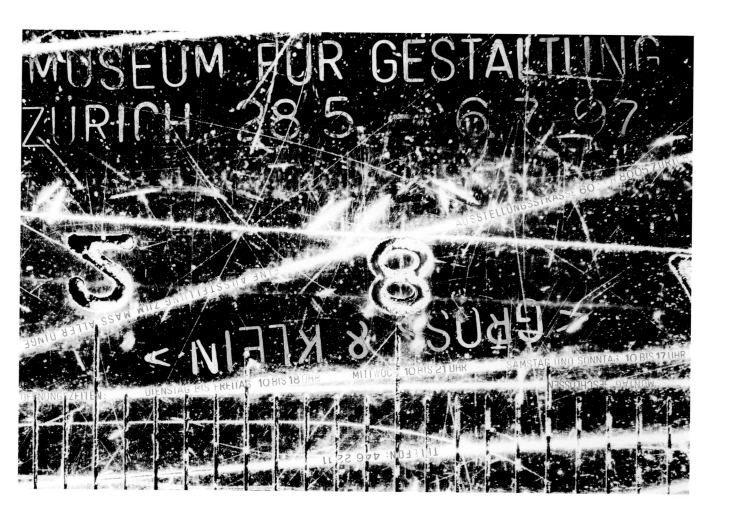

LOGOTYPE

DESIGN
Kobe and Dan Olson
Minneapolis, Minnesota

ART DIRECTION
Kobe

CREATIVE DIRECTION
Joe Duffy

ILLUSTRATION
Kobe and Dan Olson

AGENCY
Duffy Design

CLIENT
Retail Concepts, Inc.

CATALOG

DESIGN
**Carlos Segura,
Susana DeTembleque,
John Rosoue,
and Kristin Hughes**
Chicago, Illinois

LETTERING
Segura, Inc.

ART DIRECTION
**Carlos Segura and
Susana DeTembleque**

CREATIVE DIRECTION
Carlos Segura

DESIGN OFFICE
Segura, Inc.

CLIENT
**[T-26] Digital Type
Foundry**

PRINCIPAL TYPE
Various

DIMENSIONS
**12 x 18 in.
(30.5 x 45.7 cm)**

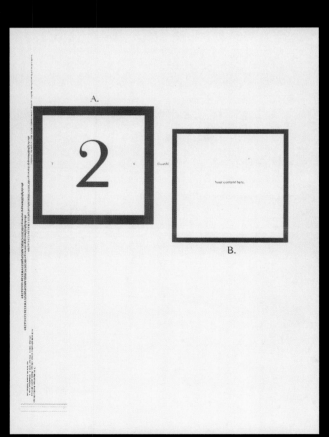

POSTER

DESIGN
**Fons M. Hickmann
and Christian Lessing**
Düsseldorf, Germany

ART DIRECTION
**Christian Lessing and
Fons M. Hickmann**

PHOTOGRAPHY
Manos Meisen

STUDIO
Fons M. Hickmann

CLIENT
**Bund Deutscher
Architekten**

PRINCIPAL TYPE
Univers

DIMENSIONS
**33¹⁄₈ x 23⁵⁄₈ in.
(84 x 60 cm)**

ANNUAL REPORT

DESIGN
Howard Brown,
Mike Calkins, and
Lance Rusoff
Philadelphia, Pennsylvania

ART DIRECTION
Howard Brown

AGENCY
Urban Outfitters

PRINCIPAL TYPE
Folio and
News Gothic

DIMENSIONS
8¹⁄₂ x 11¹⁄₂ in.
(21.6 x 29.2 cm)

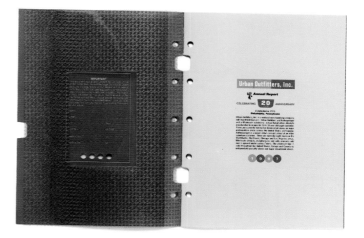

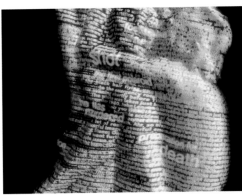

ADVERTISEMENT

DESIGN
Alex Catchpoole,
Digital Pictures
Sydney, Australia

ART DIRECTION
Len Cheeseman
and Chris Bleackley
Wellington, New Zealand

CREATIVE DIRECTION
Kim Thorp
Wellington, New Zealand

COPYWRITER
Maggie Mouat
Wellington, New Zealand

AGENCY
Saatchi & Saatchi
Wellington

CLIENT
City Gallery

PRINCIPAL TYPE
Helvetica Condensed

BOOK

DESIGN
**Various student
designers**
Pasadena, California

ART DIRECTION
Vance Studley

CREATIVE DIRECTION
Vance Studley

AGENCY
Archetype Press

SCHOOL
**Art Center College
of Design**

CLIENT
**Archetype Press
and Art Center
College of Design**

PRINCIPAL TYPE
**Metal foundry type
and wood type**

DIMENSIONS
**7 x 7¹⁄₂ in.
(17.8 x 19.1 cm)**

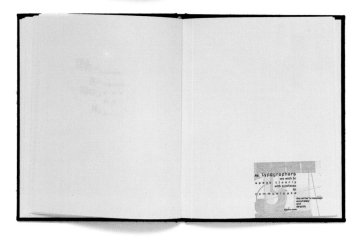

DESIGN
**Summer Powell
and Liisa Salonen**
Bloomfield Hills, Michigan

ART DIRECTION
**Liisa Salonen
and Summer Powell**

CREATIVE DIRECTION
**Summer Powell
and Liisa Salonen**

PHOTOGRAPHY
Shayne Christiansen

SCHOOL
**Cranbrook Academy
of Art**

INSTRUCTORS
**P. Scott and Laurie
Haycock Makela**

PRINCIPAL TYPE
**UltraGirl Bold
and Peignot**

DIMENSIONS
**11 x 17 in.
(27.9 x 43.2 cm)**

STUDENT PROJECT

DESIGN
Cliff Jew
Kensington, California

SCHOOL
**California College
of Arts and Crafts**

INSTRUCTOR
Martin Venezky

PRINCIPAL TYPE
**Didot and
OCRBwood**

DIMENSIONS
**8¹⁄₈ x 9³⁄₄ in.
(20.6 x 24.8 cm)**

**Second Place
Student Winner**

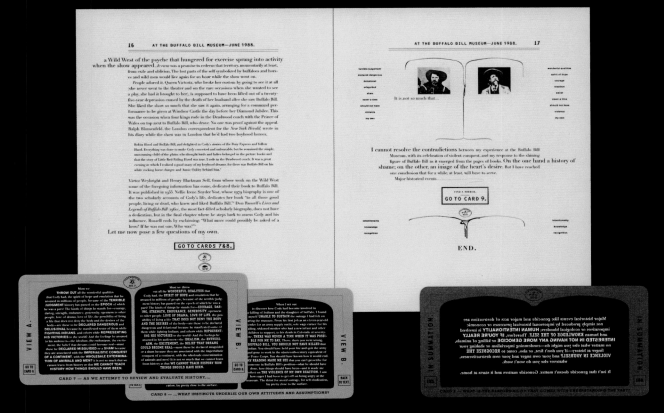

BROCHURE

DESIGN
**Thomas Hull,
Amy Wolpert,
and Jerod Dame**
Houston, Texas

DESIGN DIRECTION
Lana Rigsby

STUDIO
Rigsby Design

CLIENT
**Mohawk Paper
Mills, Inc.**

PRINCIPAL TYPE
**Helvetica and
DIN Engschrift**

DIMENSIONS
**15 x 22 in.
(38.1 x 55.9 cm)**

Is it

all linear

and

sequential?

Or is it more

like a

whole lot of things

happening

at once?

Case study two:
The Earth Technology Corporation

A $250 million engineering firm with 40+ offices across the US and
new ones springing up around the globe, promoting aggressively.

Good news/bad news: Good looking, centrally-produced marketing materials
differentiate Earth Tech in the market. But to localize or personalize them,
local offices whip up ad hoc updates and throw into a pocket folder. Messy.
Easy to lose track of. Inconsistent with an otherwise clean presentation.

What do you do? Design a "workbook" with a binding system to house
component materials. Produce high quality, offset-printed overviews centrally.
House templates for time-sensitive stuff on a server, where they can be
accessed by local offices, updated quickly, and printed digitally. Communications staff assembles the books just-in-time, throwing in an article from
today's *Wall Street Journal* (or Sioux Falls *Neighbor*.) The presentation's
personalized, current to the minute and geared to an audience as small as one.

The big question: How do you introduce consistency into a process that
involves forty offices, a couple hundred people and dozens of printers?

POSTER

DESIGN
Derek Sussner
Minneapolis, Minnesota

ART DIRECTION
Derek Sussner

PHOTOGRAPHY
LaFavor Pictures

WRITER
Eddie Prentiss

AGENCY
Initio, Inc.

CLIENT
**American Institute
of Graphic Arts/
Minnesota**

PRINCIPAL TYPE
**Bell Gothic,
Compacta,
Akzidenz Grotesk,
and Decorated**

DIMENSIONS
**21 x 26 in.
(53.3 x 66 cm)**

ANNUAL REPORT

DESIGN
**Robert Petrick
and Laura Ress**
Chicago, Illinois

ART DIRECTION
Robert Petrick

CREATIVE DIRECTION
Robert Petrick

STUDIO
Petrick Design

CLIENT
**Jacor Communications,
Inc.**

PRINCIPAL TYPE
**ITC Garamond
Light Condensed
and News Gothic**

DIMENSIONS
**10½ x 6½ in.
(26.7 x 16.5 cm)**

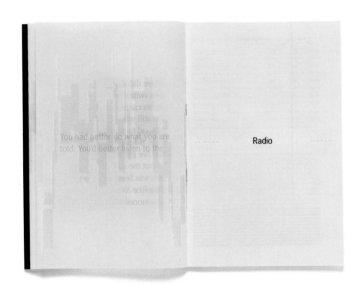

ANNUAL REPORT

DESIGN
Joe Baran
Dundee, Illinois

ART DIRECTION
Greg Samata

CREATIVE DIRECTION
Greg Samata

STUDIO
SamataMason

CLIENT
John Deere Credit

PRINCIPAL TYPE
**Gill Sans
and Courier**

DIMENSIONS
**8 x 11 in.
(20.3 x 27.9 cm)**

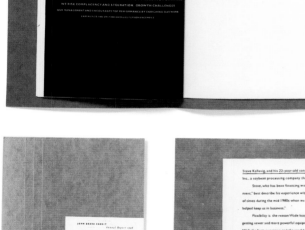

PACKAGING

DESIGN
Jason Schulte
Minneapolis, Minnesota

ART DIRECTION
Charles S. Anderson

COPYWRITER
Lisa Pemrick

DESIGN OFFICE
**Charles S. Anderson
Design Company**

CLIENT
French Paper Company

PRINCIPAL TYPE
**Custom typeface,
Alpine Gothic, and
Trade Gothic Extended**

DIMENSIONS
**Paper Box:
8³⁄₄ x 11¹⁄₄ x ⁵⁄₈ in.
(22.2 x 28.6 x 0.6 cm)
Envelope Box:
9³⁄₄ x 4¹⁄₂ x 1⁵⁄₈ in.
(24.8 x 11.4 x 4.1 cm)**

TELEVISION COMMERCIAL

DESIGN
**Kyle Cooper,
Adam Bluming, and
Grant Lau**
Hollywood, California

ART DIRECTION
Joe Shands
Portland, Oregon

CREATIVE DIRECTION
**Kyle Cooper,
Jamie Barrett, and
John Jay**
Hollywood, California and
Portland, Oregon

AGENCY
Wieden & Kennedy

STUDIO
Imaginary Forces

CLIENT
Nike

PRINCIPAL TYPE
Bell Gothic

MAGAZINE SPREAD

DESIGN
Wang Xu
Guangzhou, China

ART DIRECTION
Wang Xu

CREATIVE DIRECTION
Wang Xu

STUDIO
Wang Xu & Associates Ltd.

CLIENT
China Youth Press

PRINCIPAL TYPE
Myriamm

DIMENSIONS
22 x 14³/₄ in. (56 x 37.5 cm)

The 1994 edition of the International Poster Biennale in Warsaw has presented a larger number of Japanese graphic artists compared to their Polish counterparts. At the same time the Warsaw Academy of Fine Arts has granted the honoris causa doctorate to Yusaku Kamekura and the National Museum of Poznan has dedicated an important retrospective to the history of the Japanese poster. Meeting with Yusaku Kamekura and Lech Majewski, I ask them the meaning of the encounter between two visual cultures that may appear far apart.

Poland has given the world more than just vodka and the Pope. The poster found propitious ground here, with great names such as Frycz, Axentowicz, Bartlomiejczyk, Gronowski and Trepkowski emerging from the late 19th century onwards.

ANNUAL REPORT

DESIGN
**Rick Valicenti
and chester**
Barrington, Illinois

PHOTOGRAPHY
**William Valicenti
and Eddie Adams**
Crystal Lake, Illinois and
New York, New York

DESIGN OFFICE
Thirst

CLIENT
**Chicago Board
of Trade**

PRINCIPAL TYPE
Traitor

DIMENSIONS
**8 x 12 in.
(20.3 x 30.5 cm)**

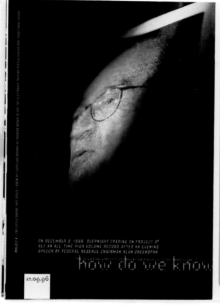
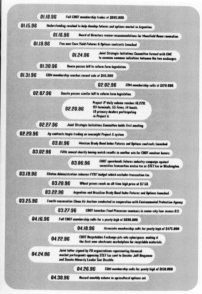
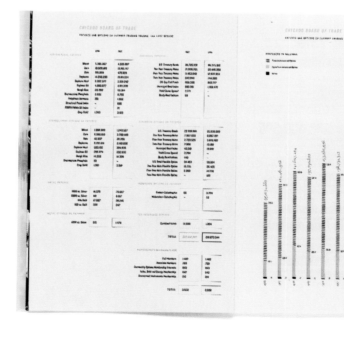

POSTER DESIGN
Wang Xu
Guangzhou, China

CALLIGRAPHY
Wang Xu

ART DIRECTION
Wang Xu

CREATIVE DIRECTION
Wang Xu

STUDIO
Wang Xu & Associates Ltd.

CLIENT
Verband der Grafik-Designer e.V. and Berliner Ensemble

PRINCIPAL TYPE
Handlettering

DIMENSIONS
33$^{1}/_{8}$ x 23$^{5}/_{16}$ in. (84.1 x 59.4 cm)

PACKAGING   DESIGN
**Massimiliano
Patrignani and
Leonardo Sonnoli**
Misano and Rimini, Italy

ART DIRECTION
Leonardo Sonnoli

CREATIVE DIRECTION
Leonardo Sonnoli

STUDIO
Dolcini associati

CLIENT
**E lucean le
stelle Records**

PRINCIPAL TYPE
ITC Franklin

DIMENSIONS
**5 $^{15}/_{16}$ x 5 $^{5}/_{16}$ in.
(15 x 13.5 cm)**

118

STUDENT PROJECT

DESIGN
Joshua Marc Levy
Edison, New Jersey

SCHOOL
School of Visual Arts

INSTRUCTORS
**Jeffrey Keyton and
Genevieve Williams**

PRINCIPAL TYPE
Various wood types

DIMENSIONS
**12 x 16 in.
(30.5 x 40.6 cm)**

**First Place
Student Winner**

SELF-PROMOTION DESIGN
Frank Petschull
Hamburg, Germany

PRINCIPAL TYPE
Futura Demi Bold

DIMENSIONS
**3¹⁄₈ x 2³⁄₄ in.
(7.8 x 7 cm)**

BOOK DESIGN
**Hal Wolverton,
Jeff Dooley, and
Alicia Johnson**
Portland, Oregon

CREATIVE DIRECTION
**Alicia Johnson and
Hal Wolverton**

AGENCY
Johnson & Wolverton

PRINCIPAL TYPE
Interstate

DIMENSIONS
**4 x 5¾ in.
(10.2 x 14.6 cm)**

POSTER

DESIGN
Fons M. Hickmann
Düsseldorf, Germany

ART DIRECTION
Fons M. Hickmann

STUDIO
Fons M. Hickmann

PRINCIPAL TYPE
Univers Extended

DIMENSIONS
27⁹/₁₆ x 39³/₈ in.
(70 x 100 cm)

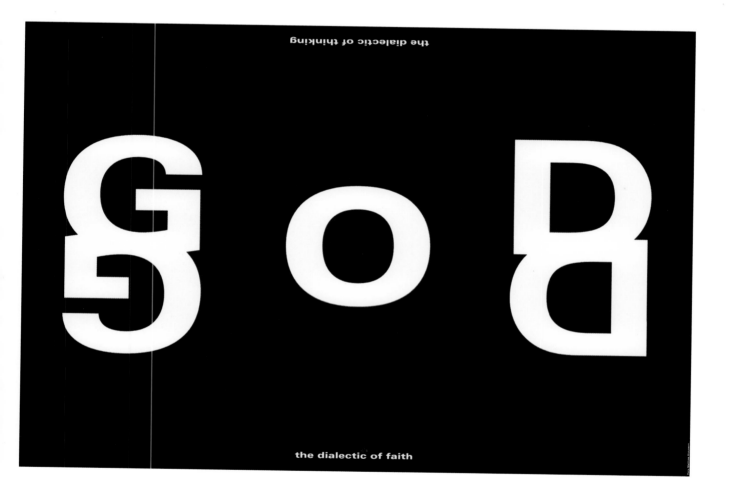

PACKAGING

DESIGN
Scott Stowell
New York, New York

ART DIRECTION
Scott Stowell

DESIGN OFFICE
Scott Stowell: design

CLIENT
**Smithsonian Folkways
Recordings**

PRINCIPAL TYPE
**DeVinne,
Egyptian 710, Futura,
and Trade Gothic**

DIMENSIONS
**12³⁄₈ x 12³⁄₈ x ⁷⁄₈ in.
(31.4 x 31.4 x 2.2 cm)**

CATALOG

DESIGN
Jennifer Sterling
San Francisco, California

LETTERING
Jennifer Sterling

ART DIRECTION
Jennifer Sterling

CREATIVE DIRECTION
Jennifer Sterling

PHOTOGRAPHY
Dave Magnusson

COPYWRITER
Tim Mullen

DESIGN OFFICE
**Jennifer Sterling
Design**

CLIENT
Pina Zangaro

PRINCIPAL TYPE
**Meta and
handlettering**

DIMENSIONS
**8½ x 8½ in.
(21.6 x 21.6 cm)**

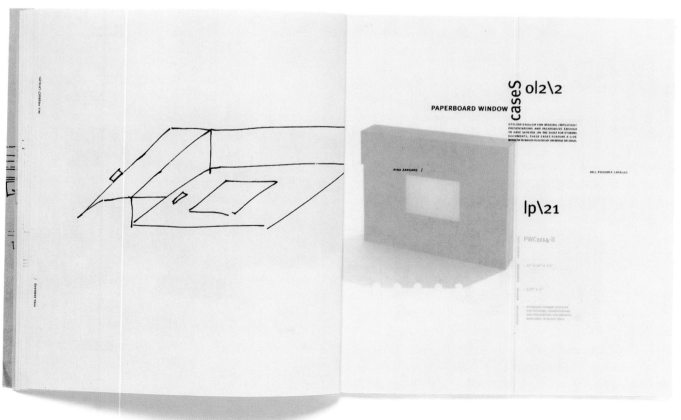

Arbeit ist das halbe Leben

POSTER

DESIGN
Ulysses Voelker
Düsseldorf, Germany

ART DIRECTION
Ulysses Voelker

STUDIO
Ulysses Voelker

CLIENT
**Förderverein
gewerkschaftlicher
Arbeitslosenarbeit**

PRINCIPAL TYPE
Bodoni

DIMENSIONS
**39³⁄₈ x 27⁹⁄₁₆ in.
(100 x 70 cm)**

BOOK

DESIGN
Uwe Loesch
Düsseldorf, Germany

CLIENT
**Verlag Hermann
Schmidt Mainz**

PRINCIPAL TYPE
**Interstate and
Univers Condensed**

DIMENSIONS
**8¹⁄₄ x 11⁵⁄₈ in.
(21 x 29.5 cm)**

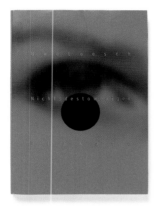

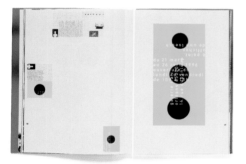

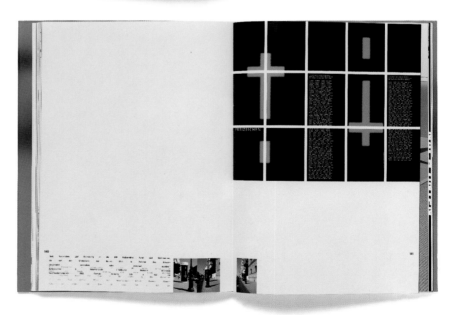

CLIENT

ELECTRONIC MEDIA

DESIGN
**Carlos Segura,
Martin Vonwill,
Hat Nugyen, and
David Hewitt**
Chicago, Illinois

ART DIRECTION
Carlos Segura

CREATIVE DIRECTION
Carlos Segura

DESIGN OFFICE
Segura, Inc.

CLIENT
**[T-26] Digital
Type Foundry**

PRINCIPAL TYPE
Various

**Unanimous
Judges' Choice**

POSTER

DESIGN
**Holger Giffhorn
and Thomas Serres**
Wuppertal, Germany

LETTERING
**Holger Giffhorn
and Thomas Serres**

ART DIRECTION
**Holger Giffhorn
and Thomas Serres**

CREATIVE DIRECTION
**Holger Giffhorn
and Thomas Serres**

AGENCY
**Giffhorn ünd Serres
Designbüro**

PRINCIPAL TYPE
Futura Bold

DIMENSIONS
**23³/₈ x 33¹/₈ in.
(59.4 x 84.1 cm)**

SIGNAGE

DESIGN
Jeff Johnson
Minneapolis, Minnesota

ART DIRECTION
Jeff Johnson

CREATIVE DIRECTION
Joe Duffy

COPYWRITER
Greg Hahn

AGENCY
Duffy Design

CLIENT
Miller Brewing Co.

PRINCIPAL TYPE
**Trade Gothic Bold
Condensed No. 20
and Helvetica**

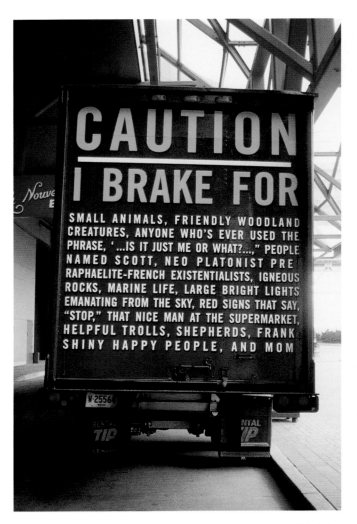

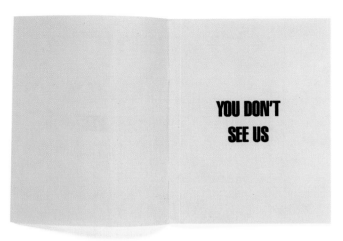

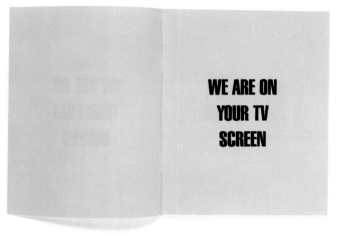

ANNUAL REPORT
DESIGN
Patrick Giasson
Montreal, Quebec, Canada
ART DIRECTION
Patrick Giasson
CREATIVE DIRECTION
Bradford Gorman
AGENCY
Behaviour Design, Inc.
CLIENT
Discreet Logic
PRINCIPAL TYPE
Helvetica Extra Compressed and Times
DIMENSIONS
8¼ x 10¾ in. (21 x 27.3 cm)

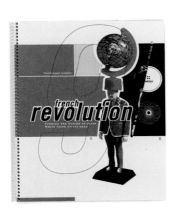

BROCHURE

DESIGN
**Jason Schulte and
Charles S. Anderson**
Minneapolis, Minnesota

ART DIRECTION
Charles S. Anderson

PHOTOGRAPHY
CSA Archive Plastock

COPYWRITER
Lisa Pemrick

DESIGN OFFICE
**Charles S. Anderson
Design Company**

CLIENT
French Paper Company

PRINCIPAL TYPE
**Trade Gothic and
Adobe Garamond Expert**

DIMENSIONS
**9 x 11¼ in.
(22.9 x 28.6 cm)**

STATIONERY

DESIGN
**Alan Hill and
Jean-Marie Brennan**
New York, New York

CREATIVE DIRECTION
Alan Hill

STUDIO
Alan Hill Design

CLIENT
**Zerøsum Productions,
Inc.**

PRINCIPAL TYPE
Futura and Scala Sans

DIMENSIONS
**8½ x 11 in.
(21.6 x 27.9 cm)**

zer sum

zerøsum productions, inc.
152 8th avenue, #4b
brooklyn ny 11215

zer sum

zerøsum productions, inc.
152 8th avenue, #4b
brooklyn ny 11215
(718) 399-2642 (917) 856-6471
bai7@aol.com

zer sum

jason kraut
producer

zerøsum productions, inc.
455 1st street
brooklyn ny 11215
(718) 965-0206 fax: (718) 965-2404
(917) 901-9552

POSTER DESIGN
**Howard Brown
and Mike Calkins**
Philadelphia, Pennsylvania

ART DIRECTION
Howard Brown

AGENCY
Urban Outfitters

PRINCIPAL TYPE
Various

DIMENSIONS
**24 x 38 in.
(61 x 96.5 cm)**

INSTRUCTORS
**Lorraine Wild, Ed Fella,
and Jeffery Keedy**

PRINCIPAL TYPE
Platelet and Trajan

DIMENSIONS
**10 x 7 in.
(25.5 x 17.8 cm)**

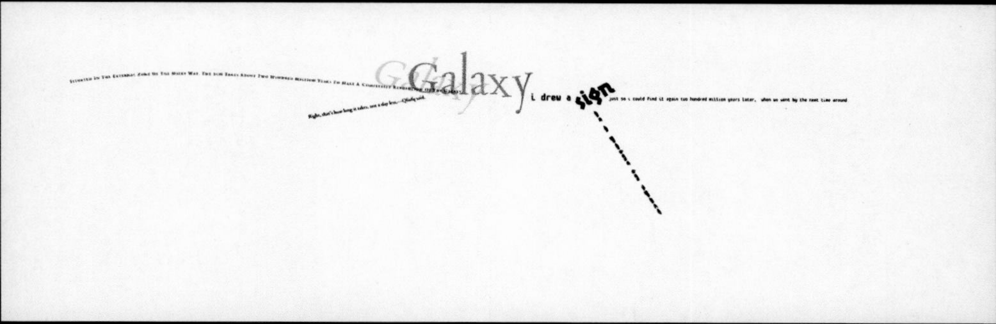

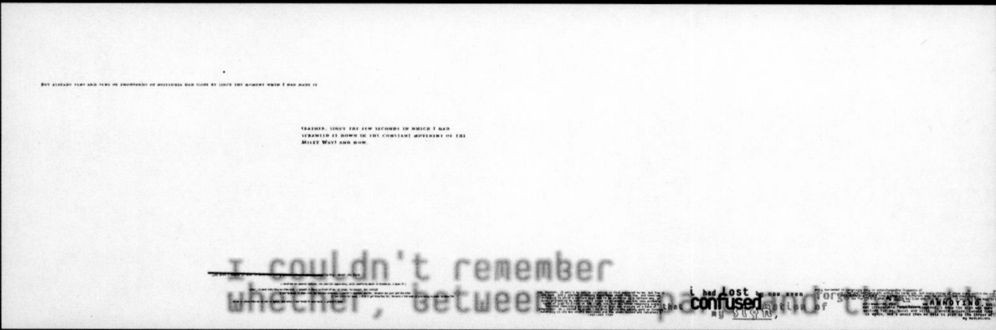

CAMPAIGN

DESIGN
Margit Tabert
Düsseldorf, Germany

ART DIRECTION
Margit Tabert

CREATIVE DIRECTION
**Annchen M. Stiens
and Gereon Sonntag**

ILLUSTRATION
Max Grüter
Zurich, Switzerland

AGENCY
Grey GmbH & Co. KG.

CLIENT
Max Grüter

PRINCIPAL TYPE
**Trade Gothic and
DIN Mittelschrift**

DIMENSIONS
Various

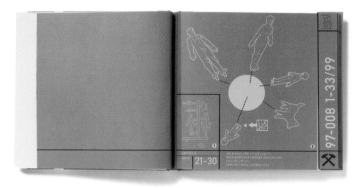

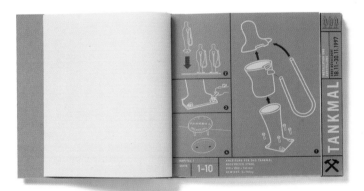

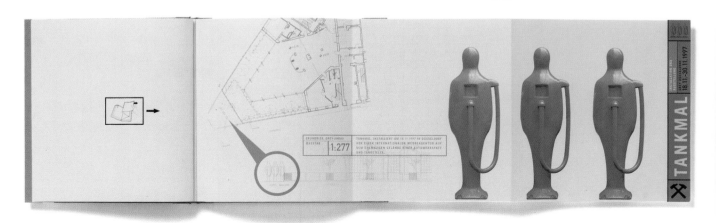

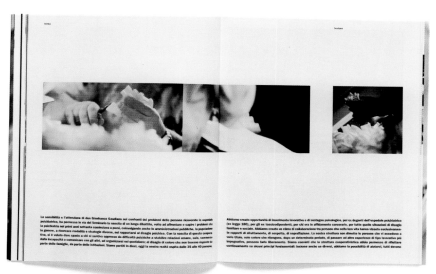

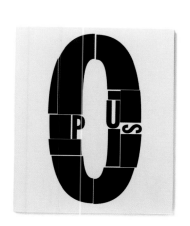

BOOK

DESIGN
**Angela Scatigna and
Leonardo Sonnoli**
Pesaro and Rimini, Italy

ART DIRECTION
Leonardo Sonnoli

CREATIVE DIRECTION
Leonardo Sonnoli

PHOTOGRAPHY
Luca Ugolini
Milan, Italy

STUDIO
Dolcini associati

CLIENT
**Don Gaudiano
Foundation**

PRINCIPAL TYPE
ITC Franklin

DIMENSIONS
**8¼ x 11 in.
(21 x 28 cm)**

PROMOTION

DESIGN
**Deanna
Kuhlmann-Leavitt**
St. Louis, Missouri

ART DIRECTION
**Deanna
Kuhlmann-Leavitt**

CREATIVE DIRECTION
**Deanna
Kuhlmann-Leavitt**

DESIGN OFFICE
**Douglas Oliver
Design Office**

CLIENT
Mead Coated Papers

PRINCIPAL TYPE
Letter Gothic

DIMENSIONS
**6 x 9 in.
(15.2 x 22.9 cm)**

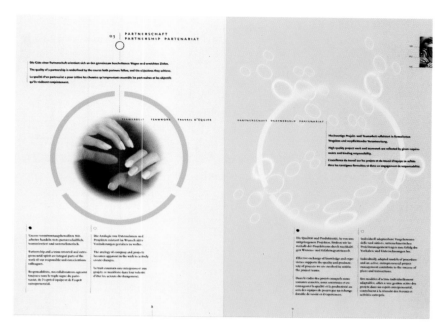

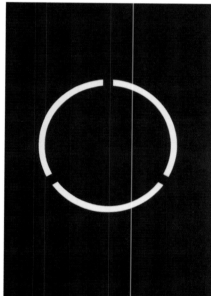

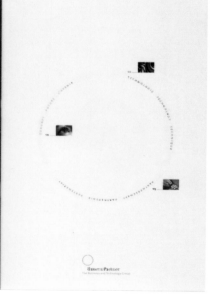

BROCHURE

DESIGN
**Susanne Effmann,
Uwe Melichar,
and Eva Ralle**
Hamburg, Germany

ART DIRECTION
Luisella Ströbele

CREATIVE DIRECTION
Johannes Erler

PHOTOGRAPHY
Frank Stöckel

STUDIO
Factor Design

CLIENT
Bauer & Partner

PRINCIPAL TYPE
Scala and Scala Sans

DIMENSIONS
**7³⁄₄ x 11⁵⁄₈ in.
(19.7 x 29.7 cm)**

POSTER

DESIGN
**Holger Giffhorn
and Thomas Serres**
Wuppertal, Germany

LETTERING
Holger Giffhorn

ART DIRECTION
**Holger Giffhorn
and Thomas Serres**

CREATIVE DIRECTION
**Holger Giffhorn
and Thomas Serres**

AGENCY
**Giffhorn und Serres
Designbüro**

CLIENT
Brot für die Welt

PRINCIPAL TYPE
**Bell Centennial and
handlettering**

DIMENSIONS
**23³/₈ x 33¹/₈ in.
(59.4 x 84.1 cm)**

POSTER

DESIGN
Dirk Wolfersdorf
Düsseldorf, Germany

ASSISTANCE
Helfried Hagenberg

DESIGN OFFICE
Wolfersdorf Design

CLIENT
**Initiative für
Gewaltlosigkeit**

PRINCIPAL TYPE
Franklin Gothic

DIMENSIONS
**33⅛ x 23⅜ in.
(84 x 59.4 cm)**

DESIGN
Renate Gokl
Urbana, Illinois

CLIENT
**Peter Lindsay
Schaudt Landscape
Architecture**

PRINCIPAL TYPE
**Perpetua and
Gill Sans**

DIMENSIONS
**11 x 7¹/₂ in.
(27.9 x 19.1 cm)**

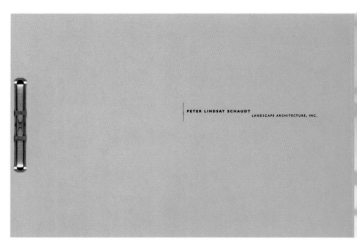

BOOK

DESIGN
Felix Humm
Milan, Italy

ILLUSTRATION
Felix Humm

STUDIO
Humm Design

CLIENT
Eva Caflisch

PRINCIPAL TYPE
**Bauer Bodoni and
Akzidenz Grotesk
Bold Extended**

DIMENSIONS
**11⁷⁄₈ x 15¹⁄₁₆ in.
(30.2 x 38.2 cm)**

OPENING TITLES

DESIGN
Mikon van Gastel
Hollywood, California

ART DIRECTION
Mikon van Gastel

EDITOR
Kurt Mattila

2-D ANIMATOR
Ben Lopez

STUDIO
Imaginary Forces

CLIENT
**American Center
for Design**

PRINCIPAL TYPE
Headline

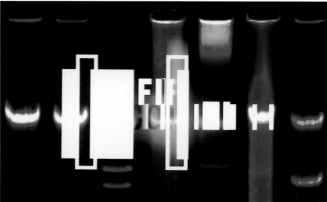

BROCHURE

DESIGN
John Sayles
Des Moines, Iowa

LETTERING
John Sayles

ART DIRECTION
John Sayles

CREATIVE DIRECTION
John Sayles

COPYWRITER
Diane De Vault
Earlham, Iowa

TYPE DIRECTION
John Sayles

STUDIO
Sayles Graphic Design

CLIENT
Jester Insurance

PRINCIPAL TYPE
**Trade Gothic LH
Bold Extended and
Zenobia Normal**

DIMENSIONS
**11 x 4½ in.
(27.9 x 11.4 cm)**

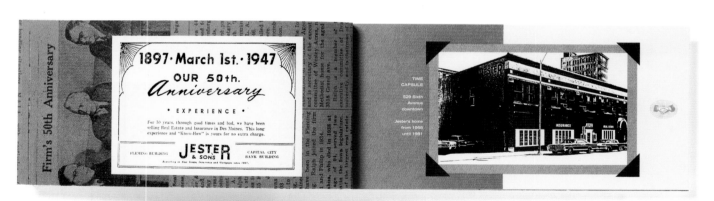

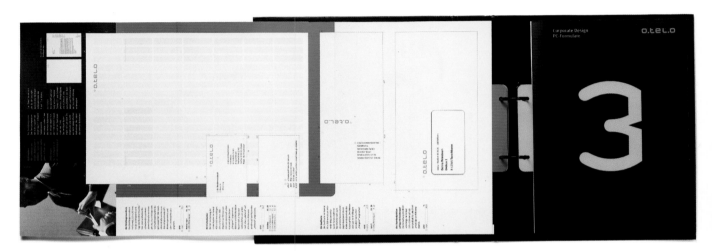

CORPORATE IDENTITY

DESIGN
**Isabella Til,
Marcus Dorau, and
Klaus Hesse**
Düsseldorf, Germany

ART DIRECTION
Isabella Til

CREATIVE DIRECTION
**Christine and
Klaus Hesse**

STUDIO
Hesse Designstudios

CLIENT
o.tel.o communications

PRINCIPAL TYPE
**o.tel.o Clicker and
o.tel.o Meta**

DIMENSIONS
**11 x 12³/₈ in.
(28 x 31.5 cm)**

PACKAGING

DESIGN
David J. High
New York, New York

ART DIRECTION
Chris Hiller
Los Angeles, California

CREATIVE DIRECTION
Julie Fields
Los Angeles, California

STUDIO
High Design

CLIENT
**Entertainment
Television**

PRINCIPAL TYPE
**Franklin Gothic Bold
Condensed Oblique**

DIMENSIONS
**8 x 11 x 4 in.
(20.3 x 27.9 x 10.2 cm)**

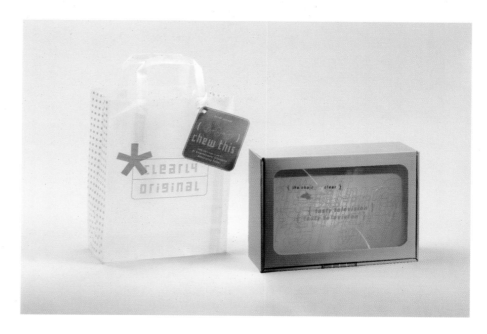

PACKAGING

DESIGN
Jennifer Sterling
San Francisco, California

LETTERING
Jennifer Sterling

ART DIRECTION
Jennifer Sterling

ILLUSTRATION
Jonathan Rosen
New York, New York

DESIGN OFFICE
**Jennifer Sterling
Design**

CLIENT
**Quickturn Design
Systems, Inc.**

PRINCIPAL TYPE
**Garamond and
handlettering**

DIMENSIONS
**3 x 4 in.
(7.6 x 10.2 cm)**

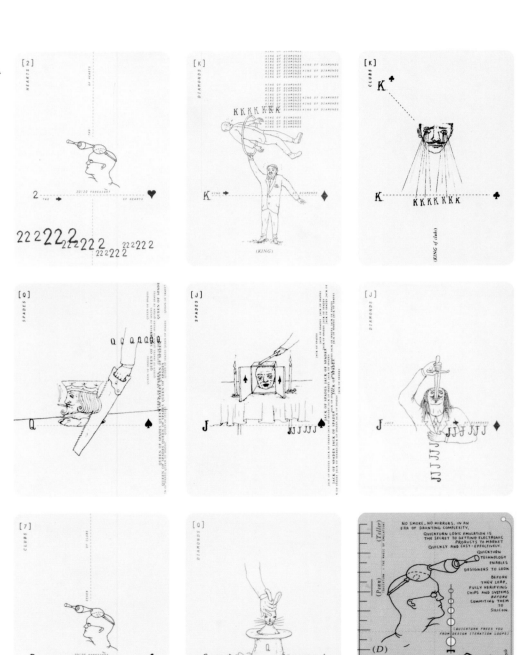

Happy Holidays*

And Many More**

**Currently under advisement and subject to change without notice.

GREETING CARD

DESIGN
**Tim Bruce,
Chris Froeter, and
Paul Bichler**
Chicago, Illinois

DESIGN OFFICE
**Froeter Design Co.,
Inc.**

PRINCIPAL TYPE
**Cheltenham Book
Condensed**

DIMENSIONS
**32.5 x 4⅞ in.
(82.6 x 12.4 cm)**

STUDENT PROJECT

Design
Adam Boladz
Champaign, Illinois

School
**University of Illinois
at Urbana-Champaign**

Professor
Renate Gokl

Principal Type
**Bembo, Franklin
Gothic, and Courier**

Dimensions
**7 x 8 in.
(17.8 x 20.3 cm)**

**Third Place
Student Winner**

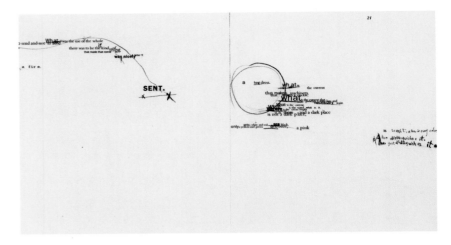

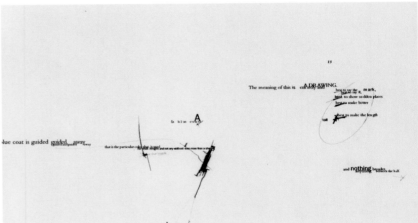

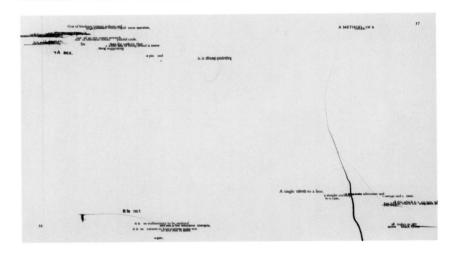

MAGAZINE SPREAD

DESIGN
Ninja von Oertzen
New York, New York

ART DIRECTION
Bridget de Socio

PHOTOGRAPHY
Norma Zuniga
Pasadena, California

DESIGN OFFICE
Socio X

CLIENT
Paper Magazine

PRINCIPAL TYPE
**Centaur Swash
Caps and Centaur**

DIMENSIONS
**8¹⁄₂ x 10⁷⁄₈ in.
(21.6 x 27.6 cm)**

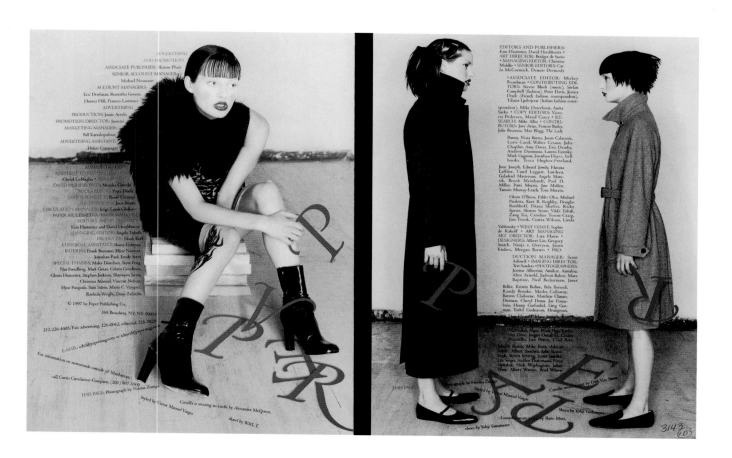

POSTER

Design
David Covell
Burlington, Vermont

Art Direction
David Covell

Creative Direction
Michael Jager

Studio
**Jager Di Paola
Kemp Design**

Principal Type
Custom typefaces

Dimensions
**25¹¹/₁₆ x 36 in.
(65.2 x 91.4 cm)**

POSTER

DESIGN
David Carson
New York, New York

STUDIO
David Carson Design

CLIENT
Plazm

PRINCIPAL TYPE
Custom typeface

DIMENSIONS
39 x 31 in.
(99.1 x 78.7 cm)

POSTER

CAMPAIGN

DESIGN
**Howard Brown
and Mike Calkins**
Philadelphia, Pennsylvania

LETTERING
Mike Calkins

ART DIRECTION
Howard Brown

AGENCY
Urban Outfitters

PRINCIPAL TYPE
**Moon Base Alpha
(modified), Dot Matrix,
and Akzidenz Grotesk
Extended**

DIMENSIONS
Various

COMPACT DISC

DESIGN
Matthias Kraus
Hamburg, Germany

ART DIRECTION
Matthias Kraus

ILLUSTRATION
Matthias Kraus

STUDIO
**Matthias Kraus
Gestaltung**

CLIENT
Ostinato Schallplatten

PRINCIPAL TYPE
Helvetica

DIMENSIONS
**38$\frac{1}{8}$ x 4$\frac{3}{4}$ in.
(96.8 x 12 cm)**

VISUAL RECORDING

DESIGN
**Matt Fey and
Kristina Meyer**
Chicago, Illinois

LETTERING
**Matt Fey, Kristina Meyer,
and Steve Gariepy**

CREATIVE DIRECTION
**Kristina Meyer and
Matt Fey**

ILLUSTRATION
Patrick Dorey

LYRICS
**Kristina Meyer, Matt Fey,
Steve Gariepy,
Sam K. Meyer, and
Allen Parmelee**

DESIGN STUDIO
Orangeflux, Inc.

PRINCIPAL TYPE
Various

DIMENSIONS
**12 x 12 in.
(30.5 x 30.5 cm)**

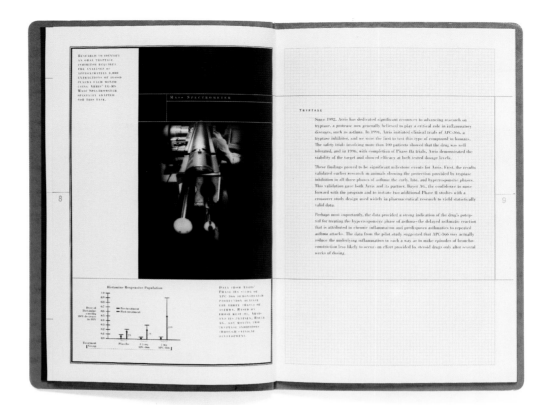

ANNUAL REPORT

DESIGN
Paul Schulte
San Francisco, California

CREATIVE DIRECTION
Paul Schulte

PHOTOGRAPHY
Jim Karageorge

STUDIO
Schulte Design

CLIENT
Arris Pharmaceutical

PRINCIPAL TYPE
Bodoni Book

DIMENSIONS
8¼ x 11¾ in.
(21 x 29.9 cm)

CATALOG

DESIGN
Charles Wilkin
Columbus, Ohio

ART DIRECTION
Charles Wilkin

PHOTOGRAPHY
**Chas Krider and
Tracy Jolly**

STUDIO
**Automatic Art
and Design**

CLIENT
**Columbus Society
Communicating Ar**

PRINCIPAL TYPE
**Folio Bold Conden
INKy, and Trixie**

DIMENSIONS
**5³⁄4 x 7¹⁄4 in.
(14.6 x 18.4 cm)**

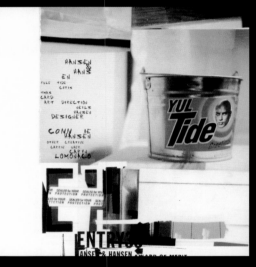

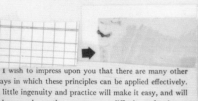

INVITATION

Design
Catherine Chesters
New York, New York

Art Direction
Dean Lubensky

Project Manager
Mary Russell

Copywriter
Thomas Cody

Client
VH1

Principal Type
Handle Gothic

Dimensions
4 x 10 in.
(10.2 x 25.4 cm)

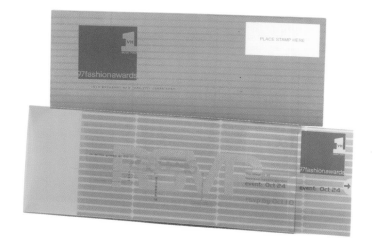

PACKAGING

DESIGN
**Eva Ralle and
Olaf Stein**
Hamburg, Germany

ART DIRECTION
Olaf Stein

PHOTOGRAPHY
**Frank Stöckel and
Steven Underwood**
Hamburg, Germany and
San Francisco, California

DESIGN OFFICE
Factor Design

CLIENT
Factor Design

PRINCIPAL TYPE
**Alternate Gothic,
Engravers Gothic,
and Mrs. Eaves**

DIMENSIONS
**5 x 7⁷⁄₈ x 4³⁄₄ in.
(12.5 x 20 x 12 cm)**

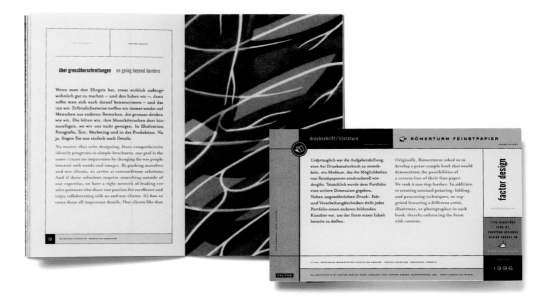

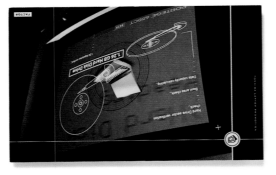

BROCHURE

DESIGN
**Rick Valicenti, chester,
and Patric King**
Barrington, Illinois

LETTERING
**Rick Valicenti, chester,
and Patric King**

PHOTOGRAPHY
William Valicenti
Crystal Lake, Illinois

WRITER
Thirst

DESIGN OFFICE
Thirst

CLIENT
Thirstype

PRINCIPAL TYPE
Rheostat

DIMENSIONS
**8⅝ x 12¼ in.
(22 x 31 cm)**

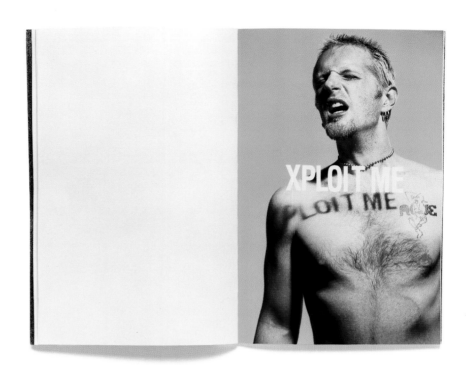

STUDENT PROJECT

DESIGN
Chien Hua Lin
New York, New York

SCHOOL
School of Visual Arts

INSTRUCTOR
L. Richard Poulin

PRINCIPAL TYPE
**Brody, Blur, Fuse,
Autotrace, and
Digitalogue**

DIMENSIONS
**24 x 36 in.
(61 x 91.4 cm)**

TRANSFLEUR

1	2	3	4	5
6	7	8	9	10
11	12	13	14	15
16	17	18	19	20
21	22	23	24	25
26	27	28	29	30
31		AUGUST 8		

CALENDAR

DESIGN
Conny J. Winter
Stuttgart, Germany

CREATIVE DIRECTION
Conny J. Winter

PHOTOGRAPHY
Conny J. Winter

STUDIO
**Studio Conny
J. Winter**

CLIENT
Bertsch/Winter/Gmund

PRINCIPAL TYPE
Scala Sans

DIMENSIONS
**19^{1}/$_{4}$ x 27^{3}/$_{16}$ in.
(49 x 69 cm)**

CAMPAIGN

DESIGN
**Howard Brown
and Lance Rusoff**
Philadelphia, Pennsylvania

LETTERING
**Howard Brown
and Lance Rusoff**

ART DIRECTION
Howard Brown

AGENCY
Urban Outfitters

PRINCIPAL TYPE
**Eurostile (modified)
and Proxima Sans**

DIMENSIONS
Various

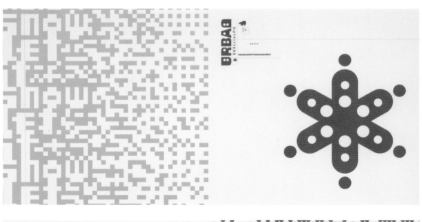

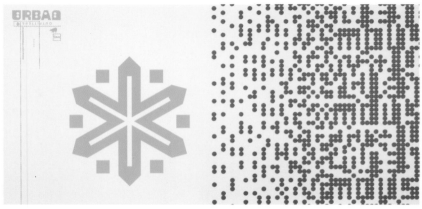

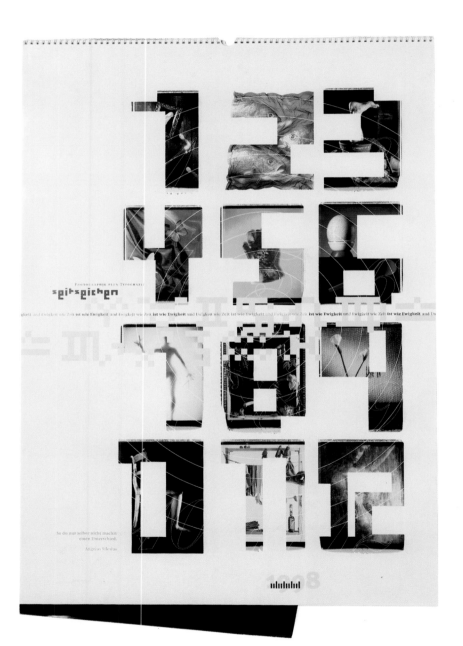

CALENDAR

DESIGN
**Helmut Ness and
Volker Liesfeld**
Wiesbaden, Germany

LETTERING
Helmut Ness

ART DIRECTION
Helmut Ness

PHOTOGRAPHY
**Tanja Mann,
David Bascom,
Martin Schlitt,
Volker Liesfeld,
Thomas Glatte,
Jörn Schäfer,
Johannes Unselt,
Kirsten Fabinski,
Dirk Brömmel,
Ira Hugger, and
Peter Chun**

SCHOOL
**Fachhochschule
Wiesbaden**

CLIENT
**FH Wiesbaden &
Societätsdruck Frankfurt
& HR Taunusstein**

PRINCIPAL TYPE
FF Minimum and Swift

DIMENSIONS
**23¼ x 34¼ in.
(59 x 87 cm)**

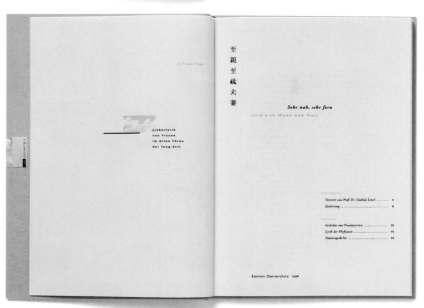

BOOK

DESIGN
**Kerstin Weber
and Olaf Schmidt**
Kiel, Germany

ART DIRECTION
**Kerstin Weber
and Olaf Schmidt**

CREATIVE DIRECTION
**Kerstin Weber
and Olaf Schmidt**

METAL BINDERY
**Schmidt und Weber
Konzept-Design**

STUDIO
**Schmidt und Weber
Konzept-Design**

CLIENT
Edition ZeichenSatz

PRINCIPAL TYPE
**Frutiger Bold,
Garamond, and
Song Ti**

DIMENSIONS
**6⁷⁄₈ x 9¹⁄₄ in.
(17.4 x 23.5 cm)**

POSTER

DESIGN
Yoshimaru Takahashi
Osaka, Japan

ART DIRECTION
Yoshimaru Takahashi

STUDIO
Kokokumaru, Inc.

CLIENT
Heiwa Paper Gallery

PRINCIPAL TYPE
OCR-B

DIMENSIONS
**28¹¹/₁₆ x 40⁹/₁₆ in.
(72.9 x 103 cm)**

PACKAGING   DESIGN
Giles B. Dunn
New York, New York

ART DIRECTION
Giles B. Dunn

CREATIVE DIRECTION
Giles B. Dunn

STUDIO
Punkt inc.

CLIENT
KAB America, Inc.

PRINCIPAL TYPE
**Pop and Akzidenz
Grotesk Family**

DIMENSIONS
**15 x 15 in.
(38.1 x 38.1 cm)**

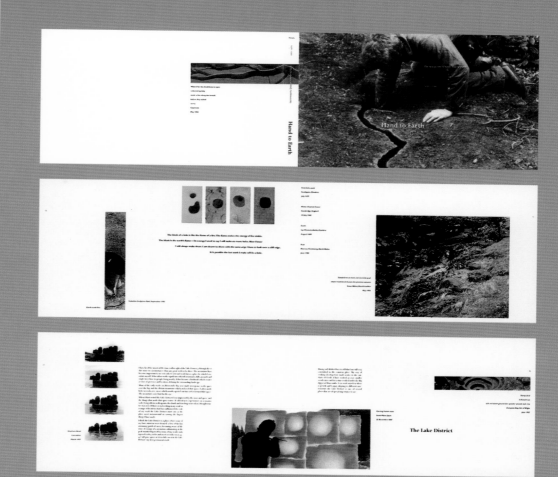

STUDENT PROJECT

DESIGN
Christopher E. Galvin
Frankfort, Illinois

SCHOOL
**University of Illinois
at Urbana–Champaign**

PROFESSOR
John V. Clarke

PRINCIPAL TYPE
Perpetua and Gill Sans

DIMENSIONS
**12 x 17 in.
(30.5 x 17.8 cm)**

BOOK DESIGN
**Rainer Groothuis
and Gilmar Wendt**
Bremen, Germany

ART DIRECTION
Rainer Groothuis

AGENCY
Groothuis + Malsy

CLIENT
Bertelsmann Buchclub

PRINCIPAL TYPE
Le Cochin

DIMENSIONS
**5 x 8³⁄16 in.
(12.7 x 20.8 cm)**

Baltasar Gracián Handorakel

und Kunst der Weltklugheit

Deutsch von
Arthur Schopenhauer

115 Sich an die Charakterfehler seiner Bekannten gewöhnen,
eben wie an häßliche Gesichter. Es ist unerläßlich, wo Verpflichtungen uns an sie knüpfen. Es gibt erschreckliche Charaktere, mit denen man nicht leben kann; jedoch ohne sie nun auch nicht. Dann ist es geschickt, sich an sie, wie an häßliche Gesichter, allmählich zu gewöhnen, damit man nicht, bei irgendeiner fürchterlichen Gelegenheit, ganz aus der Fassung gerate. Das erste Mal erregen sie Entsetzen; nach und nach verlieren sie an Scheußlichkeit, und die Überlegung weiß Unannehmlichkeiten vorzubeugen oder sie zu ertragen.

Sich nur mit Leuten von Ehr- und Pflichtgefühl abgeben. 116
Mit solchen kann man gegenseitige Verpflichtungen eingehen. Ihre eigene Ehre ist der beste Bürge für ihr Benehmen, sogar bei Mißhelligkeiten; denn sie handeln stets mit Rücksicht auf ihre Würde, daher Streit mit rechtlichen Leuten besser ist, als Sieg über unrechtliche. Mit den Verworfenen gibt es keinen sichern Umgang, weil sie keine Verpflichtungen zur Rechtlichkeit fühlen; daher gibt es unter solchen auch keine wahre Freundschaft, und ihre Freundschaftsbezeugungen sind nicht echt, wenn sie es gleich scheinen, weil kein Ehrgefühl sie bekräftigt; Leute, denen es fehlt, halte man immer von sich ab; denn wer die Ehre nicht hochhält, hält auch die Tugend nicht hoch, indem die Ehre der Thron der Rechtlichkeit ist.

POSTER

DESIGN
Ralf Weissmantel
Düsseldorf, Germany

ART DIRECTION
Helfried Hagenberg
Meerbusch, Germany

STUDIO
**Fachbereich Design,
FH Düsseldorf**

CLIENT
**Fachhochschule
Düsseldorf**

PRINCIPAL TYPE
Akzidenz Grotesk

DIMENSIONS
**45⁷/₈ x 32⁵/₈ in.
(116.5 x 83 cm)**

**Unanimous
Judges' Choice**

POSTER DESIGN
Barbara and Gerd Baumann
Schwäbisch Gmünd, Germany

LETTERING
Barbara and Gerd Baumann

ART DIRECTION
Barbara and Gerd Baumann

CREATIVE DIRECTION
Barbara and Gerd Baumann

STUDIO
Baumann & Baumann

CLIENT
Design Zentrum München

PRINCIPAL TYPE
Rotis Semi Grotesk 55

DIMENSIONS
16⁹/₁₆ x 46⁵/₈ in. (42 x 118.4 cm)

man mß sparn wo ma knn

baumann & baumann international design conference aspen usa

BOOK

DESIGN
Stefan Waidmann
Schwäbisch Gmünd, Germany

ART DIRECTION
Stefan Waidmann

STUDIO
Stefan Waidmann

CLIENT
**FH Schwäbisch Gmünd
and Stefan Waidmann**

PRINCIPAL TYPE
**Garamond, Bodoni,
Times, Futura, AG,
Helvetica, Univers,
and Rotis**

DIMENSIONS
**9⁷⁄₁₆ x 6⁵⁄₁₆ in.
(24 x 16 cm)**

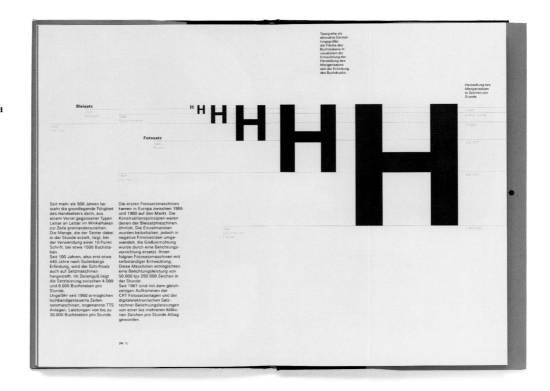

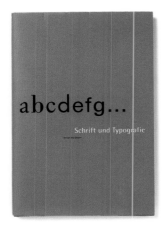

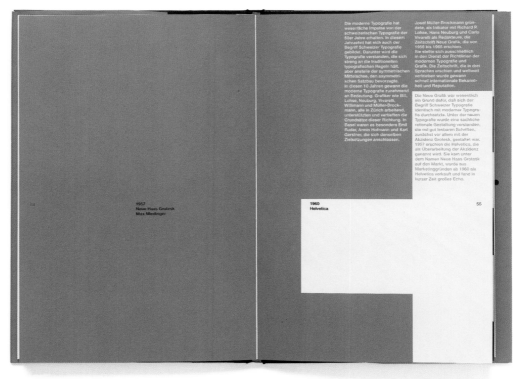

POSTER

DESIGN
Ralph Schraivogel
Zurich, Switzerland

ART DIRECTION
Ralph Schraivogel

CREATIVE DIRECTION
Ralph Schraivogel

PHOTOGRAPHY
Peter Hunkeler

STUDIO
Schraivogel Design

CLIENT
Zurich Film Podium

PRINCIPAL TYPE
Metal stencil letters

DIMENSIONS
$35^{5}/_{8}$ x $50^{3}/_{8}$ in.
(90.5 x 128 cm)

DESIGN
Paula Scher
New York, New York

DESIGN OFFICE
Pentagram Design

CLIENT
**American Institute
of Graphic Arts/
Denver**

PRINCIPAL TYPE
Cheltenham

DIMENSIONS
**24 x 36 in.
(61 x 91.4 cm)**

dare
dear,
read

design: paula scher

CALENDAR

DESIGN
**Franck Sarfati,
Joël Van Audenhaege,
and Olivier Sténuit**
Brussels, Belgium

ART DIRECTION
**Franck Sarfati,
Joël Van Audenhaege,
and Olivier Sténuit**

CREATIVE DIRECTION
**Franck Sarfati,
Joël Van Audenhaege,
and Olivier Sténuit**

DESIGN OFFICE
[sign*]-Brussels

CLIENT
Artopol

PRINCIPAL TYPE
**Goudy, Gill Sans,
and Carmella Script**

DIMENSIONS
**5¹⁄₂ x 5¹⁄₂ in.
(14 x 14 cm)**

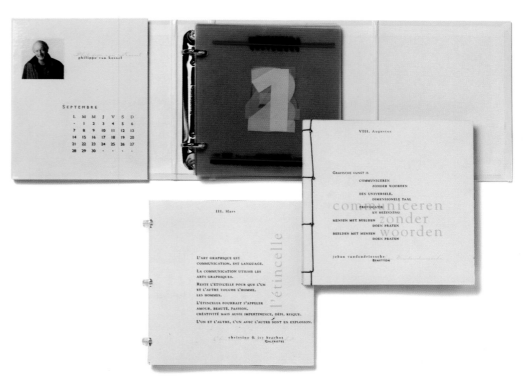

FILM BY FRITZ LANG

METRO

METROPOLIS

POLIS

COLLECTOR'S EDITION

STUDENT PROJECT

DESIGN
Christopher E. Galvin
Frankfort, Illinois

SCHOOL
**University of Illinois
at Urbana-Champaign**

PROFESSOR
Tom Kovacs

PRINCIPAL TYPE
Frutiger

DIMENSIONS
**16 x 20 in.
(40.6 x 50.8 cm)**

PACKAGING

DESIGN
**Stefan Bogner
and Boris Simon**
Munich, Germany

ART DIRECTION
Stefan Bogner

CREATIVE DIRECTION
Stefan Bogner

PHOTOGRAPHY
**Ulli Meckmann and
Marco Tabaviata**

AGENCY
Factor Product

CLIENT
Virgin Records

PRINCIPAL TYPE
**Cottonwood,
Vineta, and
Akzidenz Grotesk**

DIMENSIONS
Various

STUDENT PROJECT

DESIGN
Cliff Jew
Kensington, California

SCHOOL
**California College
of Arts and Crafts**

INSTRUCTOR
Martin Venezky

PRINCIPAL TYPE
Didot

DIMENSIONS
**54 x 20½ in.
(137.2 x 52.1 cm)**

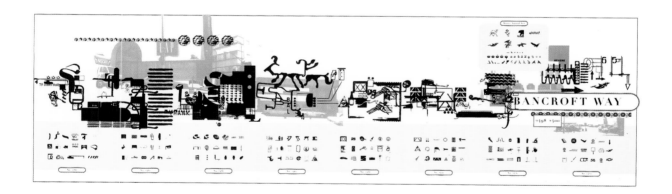

B R O C H U R E

Design
**Jeff S. Clift, Beverly Lo,
and William L. Johnson**
Chicago, Illinois

Art Direction
**Jeff S. Clift and
William L. Johnson**

Creative Direction
Wendy Pressley Jacobs

Photography
Derek Snape

Design Office
**Pressley Jacobs
Design, Inc.**

Client
Unisource

Principal Type
**Helvetica, Blur, Moon Base
Alpha, Spherize, Quartz,
and Ramiz**

Dimensions
**7 x 7 in.
(17.8 x 17.8 cm)**

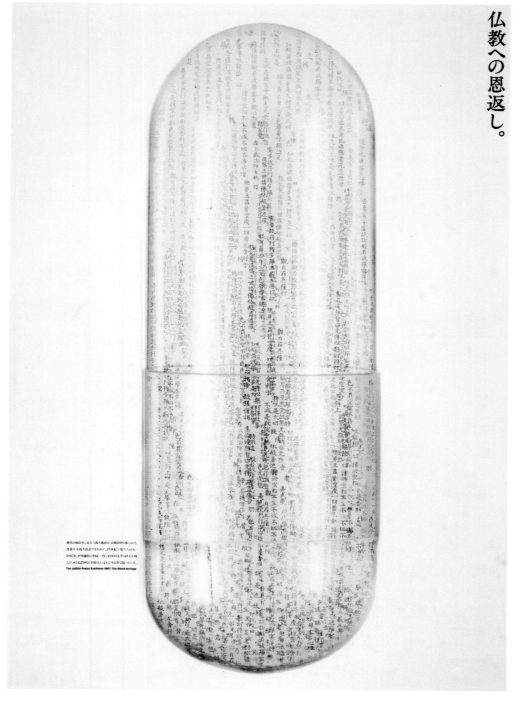

POSTER

DESIGN
**Kyoten Kimura and
Maki Yanagishima**
Yokohama-shi Kanagawa, Japan

ART DIRECTION
Kyoten Kimura

COPYWRITER
Shinji Shindoh
Chuo-ku Tokyo, Japan

STUDIO
**Rakuten Design
Room**

CLIENT
**Japan Graphic
Designers Association,
Inc. (JAGDA)**

PRINCIPAL TYPE
MM-A-OKL (Shaken)

DIMENSIONS
**40¹/₂ x 28⁵/₈ in.
(103 x 72.8 cm)**

POSTER

DESIGN
Peter Felder
Rankweil, Austria

LETTERING
**Peter Felder
and Renè Dalpra**

ART DIRECTION
Peter Felder

PRINTER
Hugo Mayer
Dornbirn, Austria

DESIGN OFFICE
Felder Grafikdesign

CLIENT
**Ton+Bild, Martin Beck-
Veranstaltungstechnik**

PRINCIPAL TYPE
**Bank Gothic and
Akzidenz Grotesk**

DIMENSIONS
**$23^{3}/_{8}$ x $33^{1}/_{2}$ in.
(59.4 x 84.1 cm)**

Damit Ihnen Hören und Sehen nicht vergeht.   Martin Beck · Veranstaltungstechnik

TON
+BILD

STATIONERY

DESIGN
Chad Hagen
Minneapolis, Minnesota

CREATIVE DIRECTION
Bill Thorburn

ILLUSTRATION
**Chad Hagen and
David Schrimpf**

STUDIO
**Carmichael Lynch
Thorburn**

PRINCIPAL TYPE
Helvetica Medium

DIMENSIONS
**8¹⁄₂ x 11 in.
(21.6 x 27.9 cm)**

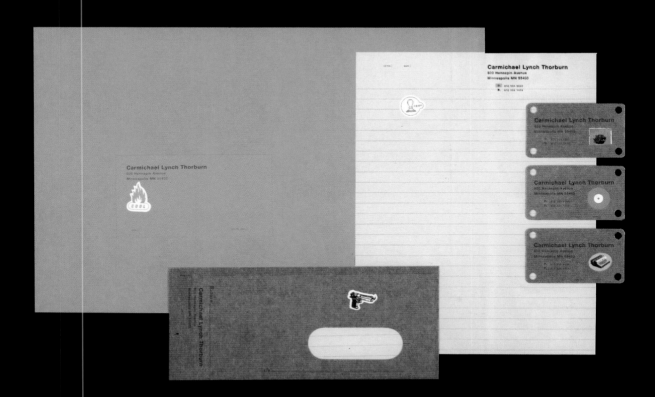

CORPORATE IDENTITY

DESIGN
Alan Colvin
Minneapolis, Minnesota

LETTERING
**Cindy Bennett
and Erik Jacobs**

ART DIRECTION
Alan Colvin

CREATIVE DIRECTION
Joe Duffy

AGENCY
Duffy Design

CLIENT
**FIFA 1999 Women's
World Cup**

PRINCIPAL TYPE
**Eagle Bold, Agency,
and handlettering**

DIMENSIONS
**8½ x 11 in.
(21.6 x 27.9 cm)**

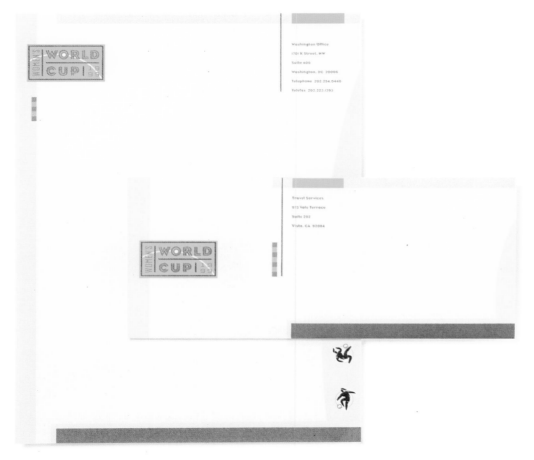

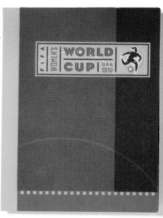

book

STUDENT PROJECT

DESIGN
Elaina Tragos
Champaign, Illinois

SCHOOL
**University of Illinois
at Urbana-Champaign**

PROFESSOR
Renate Gokl

PRINCIPAL TYPE
Univers

DIMENSIONS
**20 x 7 in.
(50.8 x 17.8 cm)**

POSTER

DESIGN
Imboden Melchior
Buochs, Switzerland

LETTERING
Imboden Melchior

ART DIRECTION
Imboden Melchior

CREATIVE DIRECTION
Imboden Melchior

DESIGN OFFICE
**Design Office
Imboden Melchior**

CLIENT
**Kantonale
Kulturkommission**

PRINCIPAL TYPE
**Univers Condensed
and Univers Light
Ultra**

DIMENSIONS
**35⁵⁄8 x 50⁷⁄16 in.
(90.5 x 128 cm)**

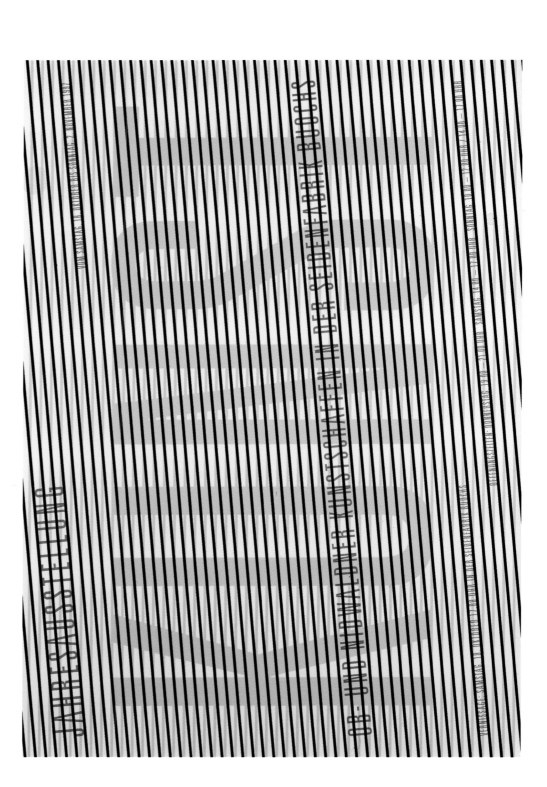

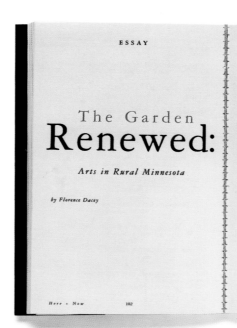

ESSAY

The Garden
Renewed:

Arts in Rural Minnesota

by Florence Dacey

Composting: It's a proven, potent transformation through a combination of organic matter, air, moisture, and light, with good soil as a catalyst. Give it time in a wire frame and you end up with the fertilizer for your next garden. You can be sloppy or fairly technical about composting, but there's no substitute for persistence and a commitment to and faith in the cyclical. The compost pile is the great equalizer, a symbol of natural economy and sustainability, a reminder that growth requires decay, and that, with patience, we can discern how each cyclical development plays its part in producing the new garden. In many ways, composting seems an apt metaphor to describe the relationships among the elements of rural arts culture, their interplay and stages of development, and the catalysts that best serve the creation of

PACKAGING

DESIGN
David Schrimpf
Minneapolis, Minnesota

CREATIVE DIRECTION
David Schrimpf

PRODUCTION
Heartland Graphics
Roseville, Minnesota

AGENCY
Independent

CLIENT
**The McKnight
Foundation**

PRINCIPAL TYPE
Garamond No. 3

DIMENSIONS
**8 x 5 x 1½ in.
(20.3 x 12.7 x 3.8 cm)**

Theater

117

und bleibe. Basta.

13 Arms ist nicht zu fassen, hab' immer ein einziges Fleckchen an-
14 pold ein. Niemand kennt Onkel Leopold, wieso nicht
15 Weiß und glatt lag das Krankenhaus hinter uns, ein Sarkophag.
16 Tupperware, sie erstickt die Speisebakterien im Keim.
17 kosteckerratten verschwinden mit langen, dünnen
18 Viel zuviel Brimborium um den Tod, er ist bloß ein

gestarrt, als wollte ich es einkasteln auf der Landkarte Ihrer Haut,
er lebt doch auch so gut wie jeder andere, den man nicht
Als ich zuhause ihren Schleiflackschrank öffnete, waren alle Kleider
Ich ziehe in meinen Kühlschrank ein, das Monstrum, das
Plastikschwänzen in Dosenhöhlen. Aufrecht wandelt der
Miesepeter, man stirbt doch nur, wenn man nichts mehr

6 ich sie aus Flachs beim Namen rufe, Stille. Als ob ich etwas in
8 ihres, gut, daß sie das begraben haben. Wäre alles andere so auf-
9 nie, obwohl es mich gereizt hätte bis aufs Blut, war im Tode, als
10 Ungetüm aus dem Sperrgürtel zurückzuerobern. Kurz vorm Tod

13 ja wohl wem gedient sein, bei Gott! Ich bin einmalig,
14 pule sie aus meinem Hirn, ich hasse, daß ich hasse.
15 immer mein Maul auf, sie haben sich in mir getäuscht,
16 wird auch der Bursche irgendwann fällig und mir das
17 schreibe sie ungern. Sie sind rund und glatt. Ich ver-
18 Aus Versehen warf ich ihr statt der frischen Nelke

einen Brunnen werfe, das nie ankommt, niemals aufschlägt, das im-
geschwemmt, hätten sie wenigstens eine fremde Frau beerdigt. Auf-
ich mich endlich drüber hermachen konnte, restlos vergangen. Die-
putz' ich ihr die Zähne, um mich nützlich zu machen. Ich dachte,

eine einmalige Möglichkeit des Daseins. Größenwahn?
Ich hasse! | Am meisten hasse ich, daß Haß nur mit Lie-
ich bin keine Überlebensgarantie, heiß laufe ich zwar,
Pfund Äpfel herausrücken müssen, zufallen wird er mir,
weigere mich der Welt als Kugel. Lieber seh' ich die Er-
mein klatschnasses Tempotaschentuch nach ins Grab.

BOOK DESIGN
Ulrich Neutzling and Gilmar Wendt
Bremen, Germany

ART DIRECTION
Rainer Groothuis

CREATIVE DIRECTION
Florian Fischer, Rainer Groothuis, and Victor Malsy
Berlin and Bremen, Germany

AGENCY
Groothuis + Malsy

CLIENT
Dölling und Galitz Verlag

PRINCIPAL TYPE
Syntax

DIMENSIONS
4³⁄₄ x 8¹⁄₄ in. (12 x 21 cm)

POSTER

DESIGN
Fons M. Hickmann
Düsseldorf, Germany

ART DIRECTION
Fons M. Hickmann

PHOTOGRAPHY
Manos Meisen

STUDIO
Fons M. Hickmann

PRINCIPAL TYPE
Univers

DIMENSIONS
**47^{1}/$_{4}$ x 33^{1}/$_{16}$ in.
(120 x 84 cm)**

STATIONERY

DESIGN
David Ekizian
Wellesley, Massachusetts
STUDIO
Ekizian Design
PRINCIPAL TYPE
Bureau Eagle Light
DIMENSIONS
8½ x 11 in.
(21.6 x 27.9 cm)

CORPORATE IDENTITY

DESIGN
Kobe and Jason Strong
Minneapolis, Minnesota

ART DIRECTION
Kobe

CREATIVE DIRECTION
Joe Duffy

ILLUSTRATION
Jason Strong

COPYWRITER
Mark Wirt

AGENCY
Duffy Design

CLIENT
Avant

PRINCIPAL TYPE
Futura, Futura Condensed, and Garamond

DIMENSIONS
8¹/₂ x 11 in. (21.6 x 27.9 cm)

STATIONERY

DESIGN
**Eric Neuner and
Agatha Sohn**
New York, New York

STUDIO
E+A Design, Inc.

PRINCIPAL TYPE
**Canyou, Akzidenz
Grotesk Condensed,
and Futura Light**

DIMENSIONS
**8¹⁄₂ x 11 in.
(21.6 x 27.9 cm)**

POSTER

DESIGN
Steve Sandstrom
Portland, Oregon

CREATIVE DIRECTION
Steve Sandstrom

WRITER
Steve Sandoz

STUDIO
Sandstrom Design

CLIENT
Weyerhauser Paper

PRINCIPAL TYPE
**Century Schoolbook
and DIN**

DIMENSIONS
**18 x 24 in.
(45.7 x 61 cm)**

POSTER

DESIGN
**Paula Scher,
Lisa Mazur, and
Anke Stohlmann**
New York, New York

PHOTOGRAPHY
Lois Greenfield

DESIGN OFFICE
Pentagram Design

CLIENT
Ballet-Tech

PRINCIPAL TYPE
Constructa

DIMENSIONS
**46 x 60 in.
(116.8 x 152.4 cm)**

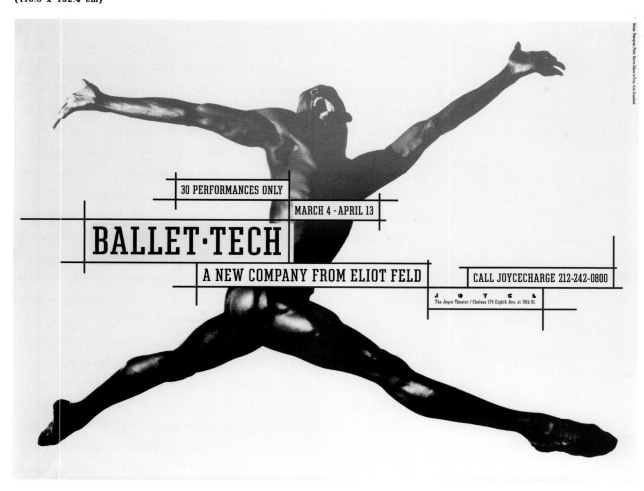

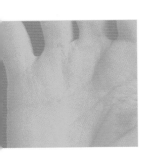

Paul Shaw, Chairman

The genesis for the Type Directors Club Type Design Competition (TDC^2) came about from my frustration, shared by the other type designers on the Board of Directors of the TDC, over the number and quality of type designs chosen in the annual competition. Prior to the inauguration of TDC^2, typefaces were judged alongside CD covers, posters, annual reports, brochures, and logotypes. Very few typefaces were ever selected and those that were tended to be underwhelming. Although many were the work of students, the rest were often no more than typographic Frankensteins— familiar typefaces that had undergone hideous digital cut-and-paste transformations. In light of the incredible ferment occurring in the world of type design in the past decade, the TDC seemed to be badly missing an opportunity to properly honor the best fonts of our time. Thus, James Montalbano and I lobbied not only for a separate type design competition, but for an inaugural show that would retroactively cover the entire decade of the 1990s. Our concept for TDC^2 was a competition, judged by both type designers and type users, that would look at ordinary text faces and wild display faces on an equal basis and that would also take into account the many non-Latin faces used throughout the world. We wanted the competition to look at typefaces not as collections of letters, figures, punctuation, and symbols, but as the building blocks for texts. Thus, we insisted that entrants submit sample showings of their faces in several sizes and leadings along with character sets. Although the format proved clumsy in some respects, it succeeded in achieving its goal of a show balanced between the workaday text faces we all use and the trendy display faces we all love to debate. The current show will surprise many viewers, as it did both James and me. Many familiar and excellent typefaces—some of them contemporary classics—were rejected. Yet, the jury of Jonathan Barnbrook, Jean Evans, Louise Fili, Alastair Johnston, and Fred Smeijers did an outstanding job. In their selectivity, they not only set a high standard for future shows, but their choices range over much of the spectrum of type design today. The fact that many popular designs failed to be chosen is a sign of the seriousness with which the jury did its job. TDC^2 has expanded the club's mission to honor typographic excellence at the source: the typeface. As an annual event it will provide a contemporary perspective on their continuing proliferation.

TDC^2 Chairmen's Statements

James Montalbano, Chairman

My idea to separate typeface design from the annual TDC competition came from conversations I had with Dave Farey while he was judging last year's TDC competition. We both felt that there weren't many typefaces being entered, and that after two days of looking at typographic/graphic design it was difficult for the judges to change their focus and look at typefaces as typefaces and not get seduced by the way those faces were presented. So a separate competition for type design, which was judged primarily by type designers, was created with TDC^2. Paul Shaw had his own reasons to separate type design into its own competition, and joined the fun as co-chairman. Not only does Paul have a great knowledge of lettering and type, he also happens to know more type designers and typographers than anyone else in New York City. So we put together a group of judges with very different points of view, created a poster that most people liked, and created submission templates that most people hated. After a lot of confusion about templates, mounting, shipping, and deadlines we received more than 340 entries that contained over 1,000 individual fonts. There were lots of surprises. Some very popular typefaces of the past eight years were not selected, but the 33 winners do represent a broad spectrum of what is going on in type design today. I would like to thank all those who submitted work, congratulate the winners, and ask you all to do it again next year.

Paul Shaw has been intrigued by letters for over thirty years. He has drawn, written, and studied them as both a designer and a scholar. His studio Paul Shaw/Letter Design, established fifteen years ago, specializes in calligraphy, handlettering, and typographic design. He is also a partner in LetterPerfect, a digital type-foundry, for whom he has designed Old Claude, Kolo, and Donatello among others. Shaw has written about type and calligraphy for *Fine Print, Design Issues, Letter Arts Review,* and *Print*. Recently he co-edited *Blackletter: Type and National Identity,* a monograph that accompanied an exhibition of the same name.

James Montalbano fell in love with type while cleaning out a California Job Case full of 12pt Brush Script in his 10th grade printing class. After taking all the graphic art courses he could in high school and college, he started teaching printing to middle school students in New Jersey. Finding his students more interested in Kiss than in handset metal type, Montalbano went on to graduate school and eventually found work in the wild world of New York City type shops and magazine art departments. After spending too much time in meetings as a publications design director, he worked in packaging until pharmaceutical folding cartons made him ill. He bought a Mac in 1989 and formed Terminal Design, Inc. in 1990. Since then Montalbano has been making and modifying type for anyone who can afford it, and occasionally releases original designs onto an unsuspecting world.

Louise Fili

Jean Evans

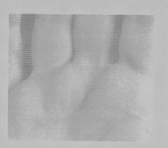

Jonathan Barnbrook

TDC² Judges

Fred Smeijers

Alastair Johnston

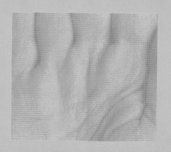

Judges

THIS IS

MASON

INCLUDED in the font are a number of ligatures
expressing often used complete words, such as
'THE' and 'TO'. A B C D E F G H I J K

L M N O P Q R S T U

V W X Y

Z

R

Jonathan Barnbrook

Jonathan Barnbrook is an independent graphic designer, font designer, and live action director living in London. He designed three typefaces for Emigre, including Mason and Exocet.

The company Virus was set up to market his new fonts, such as Bastard and Prototype. In addition to designing the cover and section dividers of *Typography Now Two*, Barnbrook has just finished work on a monograph on the artist Damien Hirst.

Jean Evans

Jean Evans is a type designer, calligrapher, and maker of artist's books. Her works appear in numerous university and public libraries as well as private collections around the globe. She has designed type digitally at Bitstream. Recently several of her type designs have been released by Font Bureau, including Elli, which was commissioned by the Houghton Library at Harvard University, and Dizzy, a design based on the handwriting of her longtime friend trumpeter Dizzy Gillespie. Before being seduced by the world of letters, Evans played on the European tennis circuit where she qualified at Wimbledon. She works with kindergartners in the Cambridge public schools, encouraging the joy and love of letters in every imaginable form.

HATMAKER, JEAN EVANS' FOURTH TYPEFACE DESIGN, WAS ORIGINALLY DEVELOPED FOR THE BOSTON-BASED BROADCAST DESIGN FIRM OF THE SAME NAME. INSPIRATION FOR THE DESIGN CAME FROM BEN SHAHN'S FAMOUS HAND-CONSTRUCTED ALPHABET. SHAHN'S ALPHABET, HOWEVER, WAS LIMITED TO CAPITAL LETTERS. EVANS' SOLUTION TO THIS DILEMMA IS CHARACTERISTICALLY SIMPLE AND ELEGANT. "DAUNTED BY THE IDEA OF DESIGNING A LOWERCASE THAT WOULD MEASURE UP TO SHAHN'S CAPITALS, I DEVELOPED A SECOND SET OF CAPS—SIMPLY, QUIRKY, YET ALMOST CLASSIC—TO WORK AS 'LOWER CASE' WITH THE SHAHN-LIKE CAPS." THE TWO DESIGNS, WHEN USED INDEPENDENTLY, ARE SURPRISINGLY LEGIBLE BUT THEY ALSO CAN BE RANDOMLY MIXED TOGETHER TO CREATE AN UNUSUAL LIGHT AND DARK INTERPLAY ON THE PAGE.

HATMAKER
ABCDEFGGHIJKLNO PQRSTUVWXYZ
1234567890
ABCDEFGHIJKLMNOPQRSTUVWXYZ
1234567890

AND LOOKING AT THE ELEGANCE OF A PAGE OF KHMER SCRIPT, AT THE HANDSOME SQUARE SANSKRIT, OR THE ARABIC, AT EARLY GREEK TABLETS, THE CUNIEFORM STELLAE OF THE SUMERIANS, OR AT THE MAJESTIC LETTERING ON SOME ROMAN MONUMENT, WHO CAN FAIL TO FIND THERE AN IMMEDIATE SENSE OF THE HAND THAT MADE THE LETTERS? THERE IS A JOY OF WORKMANSHIP THAT NO TIME OR WEATHERING CAN ERASE. WE MAY NEVER KNOW WHO DICTATED THE WORDS WRITTEN, OR UNDER WHAT CIRCUMSTANCES THEY WERE MADE. BUT THE SKILL REMAINS THERE, THE ELABORATION OF SHAPES AND RHYTHMS, THE UNDERSTANDING THAT MUST RESIDE IN THE WORKMAN AND IN HIM ALONE. SMALL WONDER THAT SO MANY PEOPLE HAVE ATTRIBUTED THE ORIGINS OF THE ALPHABETS TO THEIR GODS.'
BEN SHAHN, LOVE AND JOY ABOUT LETTERS

Louise Fili

Formerly senior designer for Herb Lubalin, Louise Fili was art director of Pantheon Books from 1978 to 1989. She has received awards from every major design competition, including Gold and Silver Medals from the Art Directors Club in New York and the Society of Illustrators, as well as the Premio Grafico from the Bologna Book Fair. Fili has taught and lectured on graphic design and typography. She was the recipient of a National Endowment for the Arts design grant to study the work of W. A. Dwiggins and is co-author, with Steven Heller, of *Italian Art Deco, Dutch Moderne, French Modern* and several other design histories published by Chronicle Books. Her firm, Louise Fili Ltd., specializes in logo, package, restaurant, type, book, and book jacket design.

Alastair Johnston

Alastair Johnston is a partner of Poltroon Press, which he founded in 1975
with the artist Frances Butler and is located in Berkeley, California.
He has lectured and written widely on typographic subjects and broadcasts
world music on the San Francisco airwaves. His latest book projects include
an introduction to William Loy's *Notes on American Punchcutters and
Typefounders* (forthcoming from the American Printing History Associates
in New York) and *The Literature of Nineteenth-century Typefounders' Specimens*,
to be published by the Printing Historical Society in London
in 1999.

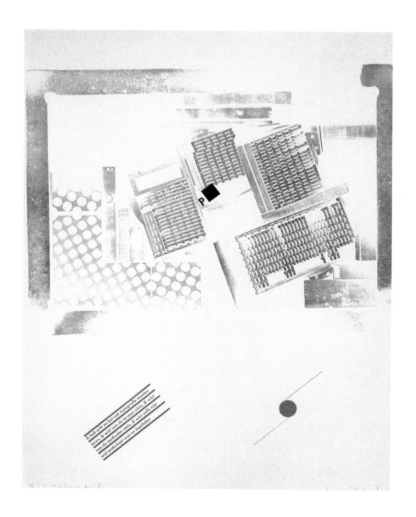

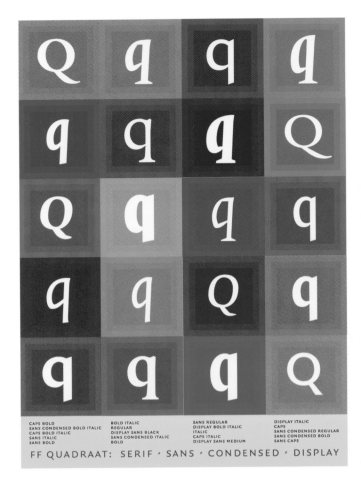

Fred Smeijers

Fred Smeijers is a partner of Het Lab. In the past he worked for Océ, where he supervised the typographic quality of laser printers, and for Phillips, where he solved problems involving screen fonts. He is the designer of the typefaces Quadraat and Renard as well as the text type used in the recent redesign of the Dutch telephone books. Most recently he is the author of *Counterpunch: Making Type in the Sixteenth Century, Designing Type Now* **(Hyphen Press).**

TDC² Judges' Choices and Designers' Statements

TYPEFACE

TYPEFACE DESIGNER
Yuri Gordon
Moscow, Russia

FOUNDRY/MANUFACTURER
ParaType Ltd.

TYPEFACE NAME
FaRer Cyrillic

SCRIPT
Cyrillic

YEAR OF DESIGN OR RELEASE
1997

FaRer Cyrillic

ABCDEFGHIJK
LMNOPQRSTU
VWXYZabcde
fghijklmnopqr
stuvwxyz
1234567890

This design is an irreverent tribute to the legacy of two important Soviet artists: Vladimir Favorosky ("Fa"), a famous wood engraver (1886–1964), and Ivan Rerberg ("Rer"), a noted book designer (1892–1957). FaRer's letter shapes also parody the aesthetics of the inscriptional lettering in the Moscow Metro (subway) stations built in the 1930s and '40s.

Yury Gordon

Jonathan Barnbrook

I did not choose this because I though it was the best typeface that was entered—it is not. But it does represent some of the things that have happened over the past few years that may not have come through in the other judges' choices. First the use of naive drawing in letterforms is a big "subversion" factor in many contemporary typefaces. Second the western European and American digital typography is starting to entice cultures with differing alphabets with the promise of exciting experiments in the future. This may in turn influence our work.

TYPEFACE

TYPEFACE DESIGNER
Tim Donaldson
Staffordshire, England

FOUNDRY/MANUFACTURER
International Typeface Corporation

TYPEFACE NAME
ITC Humana™ Script Light

YEAR OF DESIGN OR RELEASE
1995

ITC Humana Script Light
A B C D E F G H I J K L M
N O P Q R S T U V W X
Y Z a b c d e f g h i j k l m n
o p q r s t u v w x y z 1 2 3 4 5
6 7 8 9 0

Back in the late 1980s I was teasing out some spiky lowercase italic shapes using a pernicious little metal pen that I was having a love/hate relationship with. I eventually digitized these forms and married them to some racy capital forms that were loosely based on early Roman cursive majuscules. Then I wondered: *if this be the italic, whither the roman?* In response to this question these forms were drawn with a pencil, then digitized with blind mouse clicks in Ikarus M. Then I said to myself: *well a sans serif seems like a good idea.* I did this directly in FontStudio with the serif letters in the background.

Tim Donaldson

Jean Evans

The first time I saw ITC Humana Script my eyes devoured it. I marveled that anyone could capture a sensibility about shape and a liveliness so resonant with my own. It is the dancing, lilting quality that moves me. I, too, love making those second century Roman cursive majuscules that inspired Tim's capitals. The rhythms set up by the pointy lower case strokes give cohesiveness to the whole, thus allowing for a little multi-directional raucousness in between the beat. ITC Humana Script is at the same time refined and jaunty. Its thoughtful craftsmanship captures the vitality of the hand as it twists a pen on paper and pushes around puddles of ink. Lettering artists are free to tweek every individual character to accord with its neighbor, but many who design typographic scripts do not have this hands-on experience. As a result, their letters in the thousands of possible combinations within a given typeface lean less comfortably into each other. Not so Timothy Donaldson. His digital interpretation of these freehand letterforms is masterful. And to think that he can twist a pen, wield a brush, and push around a computer with equal dexterity is enough to make one drool.

Bickham Script

A B C D E F
G H I J K
L M N O P
2 R S T U
V W X Y Z
a b c d e f g h i j k l m
n o p q r s t u v w
x y z 1 2 3 4 5 6 7 8 9 0

TYPEFACE

TYPEFACE DESIGNER
Richard Lipton
Milton, Massachusetts

FOUNDRY/MANUFACTURER
**Adobe Systems,
Incorporated**

TYPEFACE NAME
Bickham Script

SCRIPT
Latin

MEMBERS OF TYPEFACE
FAMILY/SYSTEM
**A one-axis multiple
master font with
an axis for weight.
Family includes
alternate glyphs,
swash fonts, ligatures,
ornaments, beginnings,
and endings.**

YEAR OF DESIGN OR RELEASE
1997

Bickham Script is a multiple master family
designed for Adobe by Richard Lipton.
Bickham is a flowing formal script typeface
based on the lettering of 18th century
English writing masters as shown in the
unparalleled engravings of George
Bickham. In the 1740s Bickham, who was a
noted calligrapher and engraver, compiled
specimens of 24 of the best calligraphers
of his day and published them. The
complete set is known as *The Universal
Penman*. Although this work was the
inspiration for Lipton, Bickham Script is a
modern family that takes into considera-
tion the printing and output technology of
today as well as contemporary designers'
needs. In addition to a weight axis that
ranges from regular to bold, Bickham
Script also includes many alternate letterforms, beginning and ending characters,
swash letters, ligatures, and ornaments.
Fred Brady, Adobe Systems, Inc.

Louise Fili

In an age of distorted and distressed typefaces,
it was refreshing to come across Bickham Script,
not only because of its elegance and grace, but
also because it was based on the lettering of
George Bickham, whose *Universal Penman* is one of
my favorite reference books. Richard Lipton's
Bickham Script evokes the aesthetics of
18th-century lettering, yet at the same time is
perfectly contemporary.

TYPEFACE

TYPEFACE DESIGNER
Robert Slimbach
Mountain View, California

FOUNDRY/MANUFACTURER
**Adobe Systems,
Incorporated**

TYPEFACE NAME
Minion Multiple Master

SCRIPT
Latin

MEMBERS OF TYPEFACE
FAMILY/SYSTEM
**A three-axis multiple
master family with
axes for weight, width,
and optical size. Family
includes roman, italic,
roman expert, italic
expert, swash capitals,
and ornaments.**

YEAR OF DESIGN OR RELEASE
1993

Minion Multiple Master Roman

ABCDEFGHIJK
LMNOPQRSTUV
WXYZabcdefghi
jklmnopqrstuvw
xyz1234567890

Minion, created by Robert Slimbach, is inspired by classic old-style typefaces of the late Renaissance. The design comes from no single source, but is a synthesis of historical and contemporary features that incorporates elements of old style typefaces with a calligraphic quality derived from Slimbach's handlettering explorations. Minion, released by Adobe as a multiple master family in 1991, includes axes for weight, width, and optical size. The weight axis extends from light to bold, and the width axis ranges from condensed to normal. Combined with the optical size axis, which adjusts the design for each point size, Minion provides users with a wide dynamic range. Minion has become popular for a broad range of composition needs—from the extreme demands of book and magazine typography to the specific requirements of packaging, advertising, and display setting. *Fred Brady, Adobe Systems, Inc.*

Alastair Johnston

The letters of the Roman alphabet derived from disparate sources, so there is no way to rationalize their shapes, but a consistently applied theme is paramount to creating a new typeface. Novelty is not the way to make a new typeface work; a successful type design has to take into account the complex interrelationship between the letters and the articulation of the typeface as a whole. While I feel that there is no point in continuing to revive the designs of the metal era and that we must press forward with new designs suited to the new technologies, type design is a very slowly evolving, almost glacial, process. Readers require familiarity with text types. Innovation must be a logical outgrowth of the needs of communication. Robert Slimbach's Minion looks back to the metal era but does not fall into the problem of trying to faithfully recreate an historical model—something that is an impossible task since the original metal punches were cut with different results in mind, such as wear and ink squash. Nevertheless Minion is situated in the great tradition of Bembo, Sabon, Galliard, and Adobe Garamond: types rooted in the artistry of the Renaissance. The assuredness of line, the consistency of modeling and the sprightly originality of the swash italic capitals of Minion make it a durable and serviceable type, and one that I feel will last into the next century.

PT Margarit Armenian Book

ABCDEFGHIJK
LMNOPQRS
TUVWXYZabcd
efghijklmnopqr
stuvwxyz12345
67890

TYPEFACE

TYPEFACE DESIGNER
Manvel Shmavonyan
Moscow, Russia

FOUNDRY/MANUFACTURER
ParaType Ltd.

TYPEFACE NAME
PT Margarit Armenian

MEMBERS OF TYPEFACE
FAMILY/SYSTEM
**PT Margarit Armenian
Book, PT Margarit
Armenian Italic,
PT Margarit Armenian
Bold, and PT Margarit
Armenian Bold Italic**

YEAR OF DESIGN OR RELEASE
1997

The Armenian alphabet, which consists of 39 characters, was created in 405 A.D. by St. Mesrop (Mashtots). It was first used in, and obviously designed for, the first Armenian Bible, which translated from Greek by St. Sahak. The earliest Armenian print goes back to the early 16th century, and the first Bible in the Armenian was printed in Amsterdam in 1662. The current surge in demand for Armenian typefaces is due to an ongoing spread of text processing and desktop publishing in Armenian. The design of PT Margarit was inspired by the oeuvre of Giambattista Bodoni and the later interpretations of his typefaces. The glyph shapes and the high contrast in stroke weight provide for an easy combination of PT Margarit with Western "moderns" in multilingual print (e.g., Armenian-cum-Russian, Armenian-cum-English, etc.). PT Margarit was designed for use in text and display typography. *Manvel Shmavonyan*

Fred Smeijers

My personal choice fell on two designs—one that had to be from Matthew Carter and one that was non-Latin. At first I thought the latter typeface was Georgian, but it turned out to be Armenian. In the end my choice fell on the Armenian typeface. It had a very attractive kind of Bodoni-contrast without being dull or getting too rigid, which is often the case with typefaces that have a strong Bodoni-contrast. At first sight it seemed well executed and it simply looked very interesting. I do not write, read or speak Armenian, so in fact I could not make real sound judgement about it. Still my choice fell on this Armenian typeface. Although people might think that Armenian is of no real importance, this is exactly reason why, in the end, it was my personal choice. It is quite simple. I like our world big instead of small. So anything that floats not along the mainstream of fierce commercial standardization has my sympathy. This counts also for typographic freedom. This is not only about the legitimate use (and exploitation) of fun fonts, it's also about people preserving their culture and identity. Language does play an important role in that process, thus so does typography. Anyone can take advantage of the fact that written language can appear in (laser-)print easier, cheaper, and in more typographic variety than it had in the past.

Selected Entries

TDC^2 Entries Selected for Typographic Excellence

TYPEFACE

TYPEFACE DESIGNER
Christian Schwartz
Pittsburgh, Pennsylvania

FOUNDRY/MANUFACTURER
FontHaus, Inc.

TYPEFACE NAME
Atlas

SCRIPT
Latin

YEAR OF DESIGN OR RELEASE
1993

Atlas Bold

ABCDEF
GHIJKLM
NOPQRS
TUVWX
YZabcdef
ghijklmn
opqrstuv
wxyz1234
567890

TYPEFACE

TYPEFACE DESIGNER
Graham Clifford
New York, New York

CLIENT
America Online

TYPEFACE NAME
Clifford AOL

MEMBERS OF TYPEFACE
FAMILY/SYSTEM
**Clifford AOL Light,
Clifford AOL Light
Oblique, Clifford
AOL Medium, Clifford
AOL Medium Oblique,
Clifford AOL Bold,
and Clifford
AOL Bold Oblique**

YEAR OF DESIGN OR RELEASE
1996

CLIFFORD AOL LIGHT

ABCDEFG
HIJKLMNO
PQRSTUVW
XYZ12345
67890

Dogma Script Outline

ABCDEFGHIJKL
MNOPQRSTUV
WXYZabcdefghi
jklmnopqrstuv
wxyz

TYPEFACE

TYPEFACE DESIGNER
Zuzana Licko
Berkeley, California

FOUNDRY/MANUFACTURER
Emigre, Inc.

TYPEFACE NAME
Dogma

MEMBERS OF TYPEFACE
FAMILY/SYSTEM
Dogma Script Outline

YEAR OF DESIGN OR RELEASE
1994

TYPEFACE

TYPEFACE DESIGNER
Yuri Gordon
Moscow, Russia

FOUNDRY/MANUFACTURER
ParaType Ltd.

TYPEFACE NAME
Dve Kruglyh Cyrillic

SCRIPT
Cyrillic

YEAR OF DESIGN OR RELEASE
1997

Dve Kruglyh Cyrillic

ABCDEFGHIJ
KLMNOPQRS
TUVWXYZabc
defghijklmno
pqrstuvwxyz
1234567890

TYPEFACE

TYPEFACE DESIGNER
**W. A. Dwiggins
and Linotype Design
Studio**
Bad Homburg, Germany

FOUNDRY/MANUFACTURER
Linotype Library GmbH

TYPEFACE NAME
Electra

MEMBERS OF TYPEFACE
FAMILY/SYSTEM
**Electra Roman,
Electra Roman SC,
Electra Roman Osf,
Electra Cursive,
Electra Cursive Osf,
Electra Bold, Electra
Bold Osf, Electra
Bold SC, Electra
Bold Cursive, Electra
Bold Cursive Osf,
Electra Display
Roman, Electra
Display Cursive,
Electra Display Bold,
and Electra Display
Bold Cursive**

YEAR OF DESIGN OR RELEASE
1994

Electra Roman

ABCDEFGHIJK LMNOPQRSTUV WXYZabcdefghi jklmnopqrstuv wxyz1234567890

Emilida Roman

ABCDEFGHI
JKLMNOPQ
RSTUVWX
YZabcdefgh
ijklmnopqrs
tuvwxyz
1234567890

TYPEFACE

Typeface Designer
**Timothy Guy Design
and Lida Lopes Cardozo**
Truro, England

Client
EMI Group plc

Typeface Name
Emilida

**Members of Typeface
Family/System**
**Emilida Roman, Emilida
Italic, Emilida Xpert
Roman, and Emilida
Xpert Italic**

Year of Design or Release
1997

Ex Ponto Regular

A B C D E F
G H I J K L
M N O P Q
R S T U V W
X Y Z a b c d e
f g h i j k l m n o p
q r s t u v w x y z
1 2 3 4 5 6 7 8 9 0

TYPEFACE

TYPEFACE DESIGNER
Jovica Veljovic
Hamburg, Germany

FOUNDRY/MANUFACTURER
**Adobe Systems,
Incorporated**

TYPEFACE NAME
Ex Ponto

SCRIPT
Latin

MEMBERS OF TYPEFACE
FAMILY/SYSTEM
**A one-axis multiple
master font, with axis
for weight. Family
includes alternates,
beginnings, and endings.**

YEAR OF DESIGN OR RELEASE
1995

TYPEFACE

TYPEFACE DESIGNER
Matthew Carter
Cambridge, Massachusetts

CLIENT
Sports Illustrated

TYPEFACE NAME
Fenway

MEMBERS OF TYPEFACE
FAMILY/SYSTEM
**Fenway Roman, Fenway
Italic, and Fenway Roman
Small Caps**

YEAR OF DESIGN OR RELEASE
1998

Fenway Roman

ABCDEFGHIJ
KLMNOPQ
RSTUVWXYZ
abcdefghijklm
nopqrstuvwx
yz1234567890

Fritz Book

ABCDEFGHIJK
LMNOPQRST
UVWXYZabcd
efghijklmnop
qrstuvwxyz123
4567890

TYPEFACE

TYPEFACE DESIGNER
Christian Schwartz
Pittsburgh, Pennsylvania

FOUNDRY/MANUFACTURER
The Font Bureau, Inc.

TYPEFACE NAME
Fritz

SCRIPT
Latin

MEMBERS OF TYPEFACE
FAMILY/SYSTEM
**Fritz Book, Fritz Book
Small Caps, Fritz Book
Italic, Fritz Bold, and
Fritz Robusto**

YEAR OF DESIGN OR RELEASE
1995-1997

TYPEFACE

TYPEFACE DESIGNER
Adrian Frutiger
Bern, Switzerland

FOUNDRY/MANUFACTURER
Linotype Library GmbH

TYPEFACE NAME
Herculanum

MEMBERS OF TYPEFACE FAMILY/SYSTEM
Type before Gutenberg 1 containing Duc de Berry, Herculanum, and Omnia. Further TbG-volumes released.

YEAR OF DESIGN OR RELEASE
1990

HERCULANUM

AABCDEFG

HIJKKLMM

NNOPQRRS

TUUVVW

XXYYZZ12

34567890

TYPEFACE

TYPEFACE DESIGNER
Jonathan Hoefler
New York, New York

FOUNDRY/MANUFACTURER
The Hoefler Type Foundry, Inc.

CLIENT
Sports Illustrated

TYPEFACE NAME
HTF Knockout

SCRIPT
Latin

MEMBERS OF TYPEFACE FAMILY/SYSTEM
htf Knockout No. 26: Junior Flyweight, htf Knockout No. 27: Junior Bantamweight, htf Knockout No. 28: Junior Featherweight, htf Knockout No. 29: Junior Lightweight, htf Knockout No. 30: Junior Welterweight, htf Knockout No. 46: Flyweight, htf Knockout No. 47: Bantamweight, htf Knockout No. 48: Featherweight, htf Knockout No. 49: Lightweight, htf Knockout No. 50: Welterweight, htf Knockout No. 51: Middleweight, htf Knockout No. 52: Cruiserweight, htf Knockout No. 53: Heavyweight, htf Knockout No. 54: Sumo, htf Knockout No. 66: Full Flyweight, htf Knockout No. 67: Full Bantamweight, htf Knockout No. 68: Full Featherweight, htf Knockout No. 69: Full Lightweight, htf Knockout No. 70: Full Welterweight, htf Knockout No. 71: Full Middleweight, htf Knockout No. 72: Full Cruiserweight, htf Knockout No. 73: Full Heavyweight, htf Knockout No. 74: Full Sumo, htf Knockout No. 90: Ulimate Welterweight, htf Knockout No. 91: Ultimate Middleweight, htf Knockout No. 92: Ultimate Cruiserweight, htf Knockout No. 93: Ultimate Heavyweight, and htf Knockout No. 94: Ultimate Sumo

YEAR OF DESIGN OR RELEASE
1994-1998

HTF Knockout No. 26 Junior Flyweight

ABCDEFGHIJKLMNOPQRST

UVWXYZabcdefghijklmnopqr

stuvwxyz1234567890

TYPEFACE

TYPEFACE DESIGNER
Zuzana Licko
Berkeley, California

FOUNDRY/MANUFACTURER
Emigre, Inc.

TYPEFACE NAME
Hypnopaedia

MEMBERS OF TYPEFACE
FAMILY/SYSTEM
**Hypnopaedia Pattern
Illustrations**

YEAR OF DESIGN OR RELEASE
1997

Hypnopaedia Pattern Illustrations

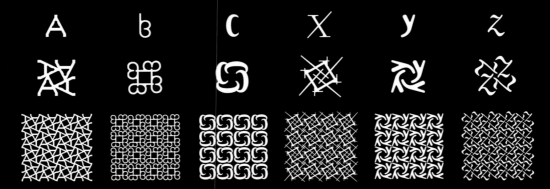

ITC Bailey Sans Book

ABCDEFGHIJKL MNOPQRSTUV WXYZabcdefg hijklmnopqrst uvwxyz123456 7890

TYPEFACE

TYPEFACE DESIGNER
Kevin Bailey
Dallas, Texas

FOUNDRY/MANUFACTURER
International Typeface Corporation

TYPEFACE NAME
ITC Bailey Sans™

MEMBERS OF TYPEFACE FAMILY/SYSTEM
ITC Bailey Sans Book, ITC Bailey Sans Bold, ITC Bailey Sans Book Italic, and ITC Bailey Sans Bold Italic

YEAR OF DESIGN OR RELEASE
1996

ITC Bodoni Seventy-Two

ABCDEFGHI
JKLMNOPQR
STUVWXYZ
abcdefghijklm
nopqrstuvw
xyz1234567
890

TYPEFACE

TYPEFACE DESIGNER
**Sumner Stone,
Janice Prescott Fishman,
Holly Goldsmith,
and Jim Parkinson**
Palo Alto, Los Angeles, and Oakland,
California

FOUNDRY/MANUFACTURER
**International Typeface
Corporation**

TYPEFACE NAME
ITC Bodoni™

MEMBERS OF TYPEFACE
FAMILY/SYSTEM
**ITC Bodoni Six with
Small Caps and Old Style
figures; ITC Bodoni
Twelve Small Caps and
Old Style figures;
ITC Bodoni Seventy-Two
Small Caps and Old Style
figures; and ITC Bodoni
Ornaments.**

YEAR OF DESIGN OR RELEASE
1994

TYPEFACE

TYPEFACE DESIGNER
Phill Grimshaw
Manchester, England

FOUNDRY/MANUFACTURER
**International Typeface
Corporation**

TYPEFACE NAME
ITC Braganza™

MEMBERS OF TYPEFACE
FAMILY/SYSTEM
**ITC Braganza Light
with Small Caps**

YEAR OF DESIGN OR RELEASE
1996

ITC Braganza Regular

ABCDEFGHIJ
KLMNOPQRS
TUVWXYZabc
defghijklmn
opqrstuvwxyz
1234567890

ITC CANCIONE

ABCDEEFGHIJKKLMMN

OPQQRRSTUVWWXYZ

1234567890

TYPEFACE

TYPEFACE DESIGNER
Brenda Walton
Sacramento, California

FOUNDRY/MANUFACTURER
International Typeface Corporation

TYPEFACE NAME
ITC Cancione™

YEAR OF DESIGN OR RELEASE
1997

TYPEFACE

TYPEFACE DESIGNER
**Dave Farey
and Richard Dawson**
London, England

FOUNDRY/MANUFACTURER
**International Typeface
Corporation**

TYPEFACE NAME
ITC Golden Cockerel™

MEMBERS OF TYPEFACE
FAMILY/SYSTEM
**ITC Golden Cockerel
Roman, ITC Golden
Cockerel Italic,
ITC Golden Cockerel
Titling, and ITC Golden
Cockerel Initials and
Ornaments**

YEAR OF DESIGN OR RELEASE
1996

ITC Golden Cockerel Roman

ABCDEFGHIJ
KLMNOPQ
RSTUVWXYZ
abcdefghijklm
nopqrstuvwxyz
1234567890

TYPEFACE

TYPEFACE DESIGNER
**Holly Goldsmith
and Ilene Strizver**
Los Angeles, California and
Westport, Connecticut

FOUNDRY/MANUFACTURER
**International Typeface
Corporation**

TYPEFACE NAME
ITC Vintage™

YEAR OF DESIGN OR RELEASE
1996

ITC Vintage

ABCDEFGHIJK
LMNOPQRSTUV
WXYZABCDEFGH
IJKLMNOPQRSTUV
WXYZ1234567890

ITC Woodland Light

ABCDEFG
HIJKLMNO
PQRSTUV
WXYZabcd
efghijklm
nopqrstuv
wxyz12345
67890

TYPEFACE

TYPEFACE DESIGNER
Akira Kobayashi
Tokyo, Japan

FOUNDRY/MANUFACTURER
**International Typeface
Corporation**

TYPEFACE NAME
ITC Woodland™

MEMBERS OF TYPEFACE
FAMILY/SYSTEM
**ITC Woodland Light,
ITC Woodland Medium,
ITC Woodland Demi,
and ITC Woodland Black**

YEAR OF DESIGN OR RELEASE
1997

Journal Text

ABCDEFGHIJKLMN
OPQRSTUVWXYZ
abcdefghijklmno
pqrstuvwxyz

TYPEFACE

TYPEFACE DESIGNER
Zuzana Licko
Berkeley, California

FOUNDRY/MANUFACTURER
Emigre, Inc.

TYPEFACE NAME
Journal

MEMBERS OF TYPEFACE
FAMILY/SYSTEM
**Journal Text, Journal
Italic, and Journal Ultra**

YEAR OF DESIGN OR RELEASE
1990

ff Meta Plus Roman

ABCDEFGH
IJKLMNOPQ
RSTUVWXY
Zabcdefghi
jklmnopqrs
tuvwxyz123
4567890

TYPEFACE

TYPEFACE DESIGNER
Erik Spiekermann
Berlin, Germany

FOUNDRY/MANUFACTURER
**FontShop International
(FSI)**

TYPEFACE NAME
ff Meta Plus™

MEMBERS OF TYPEFACE
FAMILY/SYSTEM
**ff Meta Plus Roman,
ff Meta Plus Caps, ff Meta
Plus Italic, ff Meta Plus
Italic Caps, ff Meta Plus
Book, ff Meta Plus Book
Italic, ff Meta Plus Book
Caps, ff Meta Plus Book
Italic Caps, ff Meta Plus
Medium, ff Meta Plus
Medium Italic, ff Meta Plus
Medium Caps, ff Meta Plus
Medium Italic Caps,
ff Meta Plus Bold, ff Meta
Plus Bold Italic, ff Meta
Plus Bold Italic Caps,
ff Meta Plus Black, and
ff Meta Plus Black Italic**

YEAR OF DESIGN OR RELEASE
1993

NYX

ABCDEFGHIJKLM
NOPQRSTUVWXYZ
1234567890

TYPEFACE

TYPEFACE DESIGNER
Riek Cusiek
Overland Park, Kansas

FOUNDRY/MANUFACTURER
**Adobe Systems,
Incorporated**

TYPEFACE NAME
NYX

YEAR OF DESIGN OR RELEASE
1997

TYPEFACE

TYPEFACE DESIGNER
**Scott-Martin Kosofsky
(after Richard Austin,
London, 1788)**
Boston, Massachusetts

TYPEFACE NAME
Philidor Bell-Text

MEMBERS OF TYPEFACE
FAMILY/SYSTEM
**Philidor Bell-Text Roman,
Philidor Bell-Text Italic,
and Philidor Bell-Text
Small Caps**

YEAR OF DESIGN OR RELEASE
1995

Philidor Bell-Text Roman

ABCDEFGH
IJKLMNOPQ
RSTUVWX
YZabcdefghij
klmnopqrstu
vwxyz123456
7890

להללטח צסדטלטחע
(Philidor Hillel)

יטחזוהדגבא
קצפעסנמלכ
רשת‖‖12345
67890

TYPEFACE · TYPEFACE DESIGNER
Scott-Martin Kosofsky
Boston, Massachusetts

TYPEFACE NAME
Philidor Hillel

SCRIPT
Hebrew

YEAR OF DESIGN OR RELEASE
1991

TYPEFACE

TYPEFACE DESIGNER
Lyubov Kuznetsova
Moscow, Russia

FOUNDRY/MANUFACTURER
ParaType Ltd.

TYPEFACE NAME
PT Kufi Arabic

SCRIPT
Arabic

MEMBERS OF TYPEFACE
FAMILY/SYSTEM
**PT Kufi Arabic Light,
PT Kufi Arabic Light
Oblique, PT Kufi Arabic
Regular, PT Kufi Arabic
Regular Oblique,
PT Kufi Arabic Bold,
and PT Kufi Arabic
Bold Oblique**

YEAR OF DESIGN OR RELEASE
1997

ت ثـ بـهآبـ بآثاباأ

(PT Kufi Arabic Regular)

ت تـ تتبـ بـ بيبإإأأآآآاااا

ثـ ثـ ثحجـ جـ جمهـهفـفخ

خ خد د ذذرر زز نـ سـ سس

سـ شـ شـ شـ شـ شـ شـ شـطـ

١٢٣٤٥ طـ طصصضظظظا

٦٧٨٩٠

SHOWCARD GOTHIC

ABCDEFGHI
JKLMNOPQ
RSTUVWXY
Z1234567890

TYPEFACE

TYPEFACE DESIGNER
Jim Parkinson
Oakland, California

FOUNDRY/MANUFACTURER
The Font Bureau, Inc.

TYPEFACE NAME
Showcard Gothic

YEAR OF DESIGN OR RELEASE
1993

TYPEFACE TYPEFACE DESIGNER
Nina David
Ratingen, Germany
TYPEFACE NAME
UniF
YEAR OF DESIGN OR RELEASE
1997

unif

ABCDEFGHIJK
LMNOPQRSTUV
WXYZ

Volgare Primo

A B C D E F G H I

J K L M N O P Q

R S T U V W X Y Z

Z a b c d e f g h i j k l m n o p

q r s t u v w x y Z 1 2 3 4

5 6 7 8 9 0

TYPEFACE

Typeface Designer
Stephen Farrell
Chicago, Illinois

Foundry/Manufacturer
The Mss Folio

Typeface Name
Volgare

Members of Typeface
Family/System
**Volgare Primo,
Volgare Secondo,
and Volgare Terzo**

Year of Design or Release
1996